The Horse in My Garage

and Other Stories

The Horse in My Garage

AND OTHER STORIES

by
Patrick F. McManus

Skyhorse Publishing

Skyhorse Publishing books may be purchased in bulk
at special discounts for sales promotion, corporate gifts,
fund-raising, or educational purposes. Special editions can
also be created to specifications. For details, contact the
Special Sales Department, Skyhorse Publishing,
307 West 36th Street, 11th Floor, New York,
NY 10018 or info@skyhorsepublishing.com.

Skyhorse® and Skyhorse Publishing® are registered
trademarks of Skyhorse Publishing, Inc.®,
a Delaware corporation.

Visit our website at www.skyhorsepublishing.com

10 9 8

Library of Congress Cataloging-in-Publication Data
is available on file.

ISBN: 978-1-62636-117-1

Printed in China

Contents

Preface   vii

A Scholar of Worms   1

Shaping Up for the Hunt   7

A Bit about My Writing Life   15

Big   23

$7,000 TV Historical Extravaganza   29

Wild Life in a Room with a View   35

Risk Assessment   47

The Forty-Pound Brown Trout   55

Bear Hunters   61

A Lake Too Far   71

The Chicken Chronicles   77

Secret Athlete   81

Contents

The McManus Principles   85

Basic Lying Made Easy   89

A Chainsaw Kind of Guy   97

The Lady Who Kept Things   103

September Song   109

The Longest March   115

The Stalk   119

The Horse in My Garage   125

The Tent   131

To Smoke a Steelhead   135

The Teachings of Rancid Crabtree   141

Christmas Shopping   147

Who Ate My Shakespeare?   151

Romantic Moments   155

The Canoe   159

The Writing of "The Green Box"   165

A Routine Fishing Trip   169

The Brown Pelican   173

Canoodled   177

Christmas Over Easy   183

Dog People   189

Finding My Roots   193

The Longest Three Miles   197

Scrabble's Powers of Observation   201

The Dark and Other Dangers   205

Preface

One day, as a freshman at Washington State College (now University), I was browsing through the magazine section of Holland Library and came across two magazines aimed at writers and would-be writers. It was at that moment I discovered there was such a thing as freelance writing. That's for me, I thought. I couldn't imagine an employer dumb enough to hire me, and I wouldn't want to work for somebody that dumb anyway. But here was a form of work where one could be his own boss. It never occurred to me that I would still be working for someone pretty dumb.

From then on I began writing features for magazines and newspapers. By the time I graduated from college, I had sold dozens of features. Typically, I was paid $25 for a piece, but there were lots of cheap publications around, too. Still, I loved the work, regardless of the rate of pay. Eventually, I was hired by Eastern Washington State College of Education (now Eastern Washington University) as an instructor in journalism. I had summers off to devote my time entirely to freelancing.

All of the stories I wrote in those early years were factual. Two of the factual articles are included in this collection and pretty much represent the high point of my article writing. Even though both are factual, I think the one thing that distinguishes them is that each has a touch of humor. One is "Wild Life in a Room with a View," originally published by *Sports Illustrated* and later abridged by *Reader's Digest*. The other is "$7,000 Television Extravaganza," published by *TV Guide*.

During this period, I wrote every night for two hours, seven nights a week, and I tried never to miss a writing session or to cut one short. One night, in the first hour of my two-hour session, I finished an article on the use of telemetry in the study of wildlife, whereby wild animals are hooked up with radio transmitters so scientists can follow their travels at night. I finished writing the article in the first hour of my session and still had an hour to go. So I decided to write a piece of nonsense to fill up my last hour. The idea for the piece was that eventually all animals will be equipped with radios, and this will simplify hunting a great deal. As was my practice at the time, anything I wrote I sent off to a magazine. This piece went to *Field & Stream*, because it touched on hunting. One day I went out to the mailbox, and there was a small envelope from *Field & Stream*. Freelance writers tend to get excited over small envelopes as opposed to large envelopes. Large envelopes contain the rejected manuscript, and small envelopes contain checks. I ripped open the small envelope and it contained a check for $350! Now I had just sold a factual article for $750, but it had taken me a month to research and write. This piece of nonsense had taken me an hour! At that instant, I became a humor writer.

Also included in this collection is my very first published fiction, "The Lady Who Kept Things." I wrote it in a creative writing class, and it was later published in *SPARK*, the student literary magazine at WSU. The instructor never thought much of my writing and refused to give me a grade higher than a B. We often had to read a story aloud to the class, and one day I read one of my humor pieces. The class laughed themselves sick. Even the instructor had to take off his glasses and wipe away tears of mirth. Back came the paper, with a grade of B! I stormed into the professor's office and cried, "How could you give me a grade of B on this story when the class loved it and even you had to wipe away tears?" He said, "Yes, McManus, it was a very funny story, but this is a class in the writing of serious literature, and you have to admit that story wasn't serious."

I offer this as a word of warning to anyone interested in a career as a humor writer. Indeed, once I received a letter from an editor, asking me to write for his magazine. "But not humor," he said. "It's too dangerous." Yeah, well, he should try writing it.

A final note: You may come across in reading this collection of stories and essays a few repetitions of subjects, ideas and experiences. Let me explain how they and this book came about.

In the corner of one of the closets in our business office, I came across a high stack of file folders with a sign on top that said "Stories not collected in books." Well, I said to myself, it would be a shame not to put these stories into their own book. I did not realize the complexities involved in this undertaking. The stories had been written over a period of fifty years, say from when I was twenty-nine to my present age of seventy-nine. None of my other collections contained stories written over such a span of time. Most were reprinted from *Outdoor Life* and *Field & Stream*, each collection covering stories from a period of no more than two or three years. In this book, however, two stories could be separated by as many as fifty years. In writing the second story I probably had forgotten the first story, and somehow managed to repeat some material. I think the editors and I have managed to catch the most grievous repetitions, but, if you should come across one, perhaps you would be kind enough to view it as an archaeological find, in other words a gold nugget, in the drifting sands of a failing memory. P. M.

A Scholar of Worms

My wife brought a neat little metal box into my office the other day and asked, "Wouldn't this be good for worms?"

I looked at the box. It would fit nicely in a shirt or vest pocket. The latch on it opened easily. You could hold it out toward a fishing partner, snap it open, and ask, "Worm?" I figured it was about big enough for four worms at a time. It would work well if your fishing buddy carried a big can of worms, and you could meet him from time to time for a refill, kind of like fighter planes meeting a tanker in mid-flight to get a refill.

"Perfect!" I said.

Actually, I couldn't remember the last time I had fished with worms. Maggots, yes—worms, no. Worms were starting to become a distant memory. The thought saddened me, because I'd once been a scholar of worms.

My very first worm scared me half to death. I was four or five years old and digging in the dirt at the corner of our ancient log cabin. Dirt, at the time, was my favorite toy, possibly my only toy. I forget what I used for a digging tool, perhaps an old spoon my mother had given me. I was soon working on a major excavation. That is how you play with dirt; you move it from one place to another. Suddenly, I unearthed a huge night crawler. It had never occurred to me that a worm could be so large. I thought it was a snake.

I went into the cabin to report my find, something I by then viewed as a scientific discovery.

"Don't rip the door off its hinges!" Mom shouted. "Stop that screeching and shaking dirt all over the floor." (My mother had very little experience with scientists.)

I pulled her outside to show her the snake and was pleased to learn my discovery was only a worm. Still, for several years, I was not particularly fond of night crawlers. They kind of ruined dirt for me. Afterward, I only dug in the dirt tentatively, always expecting the next spoonful to turn up another monster. I preferred worms with fewer pretensions, something a bit more modest.

As mentioned, I have in recent years used mostly maggots for bait. True, they lack the worm's personality and character, but on the other hand they are rather tidy, not counting the wood shavings vendors typically use as fillers in their plastic containers. I suppose maggots, technically speaking, are worms of a sort. If you have gathered maggots from their natural medium, you will think their plastic containers one of the great inventions of mankind. You will not mind in the least vacuuming up from the floor of your boat the wood shavings and the little brown corpses of escaped maggots. (What were they thinking, anyway? That they could make a run for it?) Another thing I like about fishing with maggots is that if left alone they turn into flies. What kind of future is that for them? You have saved them from that particular horror, for which they should thank you copiously. At least a worm has the self-respect to remain a worm. Kind of reminds me of a couple of kids I knew in high school, not that I'm promoting any shortcomings of self-respect.

A couple of years after the discovery of my first night crawler, we moved back to our farm in Idaho. We raised mostly stumps on our farm. They tended to mind their own business and didn't cause much trouble, such as whining to be harvested. Then my parents lapsed into insanity and started populating the farm with cows, pigs, chickens, rabbits, and other irritants. Our former tranquil life in the woods was suddenly transformed into endless emergencies, perpetrated by these useless and irresponsible new residents.

On its plus side, the farm came with a creek. The creek was a mess. It had high walls of brush hugging its banks, logs crisscrossing it, beaver dams backing up the water, and huge cedar stumps disrupting the current. It was lovely. Sometimes during runoff, ice would catch on the logs and form huge dams. Once, the water rose so high behind one dam that it almost took out the barn and its livestock. But no such luck.

The creek, or "crick," as we referred to it in those days, was wild and unpredictable, much like my own character at the time. Even though the creek harbored mostly chaos, it also contained in its deep dark holes an abundance of hungry trout. Those trout changed my life. Had I not discovered them, I might have grown up to become . . . well, I might have grown up.

In my pre-creek years, I thought of worms as primarily useless, if occasionally entertaining, in the way only worms can be. Once I realized worms could be used to catch fish, I began to study them closely and soon became a scholar of worms. I read everything I could find written about worms. OK, I'll admit it, not all that much was written about worms.

In the spring of the year, before fishing season opened, worms were plentiful. They lay around on the top of the ground sunning themselves or, often, drowning in puddles, getting themselves squished under vehicle tires, and otherwise acting stupidly. Those wisely remaining underground could be clever, inventing numerous escapes from my flailing shovel. Sometimes I would notice the rear tip of one disappearing into the bottom of my excavation. Despite my making the dirt fly, I could never seem to catch up with the worm. It was as if it knew of secret worm speedways routed through the dirt.

Sensing the arrival of fishing season, all worms, even the dumb ones, began burrowing deep in the earth. Usually, the best place to dig worms was in what we laughingly called "the garden." Each spring we would spade up the ground and plant numerous seeds, with visions of squash, pumpkins, lettuce, onions, and potatoes dancing in our heads. I vaguely recall some of the plants actually reaching a height of two inches or more before drying up and dying. It was that garden that first taught me the futility of hope. Nevertheless, the garden soil had been loosened, and that made it fairly easy to turn up a dozen or so worms in a fairly short time, at least in the months of May and June. One spring, having experienced a dearth of midsummer worms in previous years, I dug up several dozen worms and saved them in a large box of dirt. I had been told that worms like coffee grounds, so I dumped in a bunch of grounds to provide them with nourishment. Come July, when other worms had dug themselves halfway to China, I went out to the box, smugly anticipating great wiggly handfuls of its contents. Apparently high on caffeine, the worms had gone over the walls en masse. ("The next moonless night—*hic*—we make our break. Pass it along.") No matter the cause of the inmates' disappearance, I blamed the coffee grounds. Never again did I try to store up worms.

Fortunately, we had a huge pile of cow manure out behind our barn, and worms could be found there any time of the year. They were pale, skinny fellows, as you might expect of anyone who lived in a manure pile. The fish in the creek, however, did not seem to care much for manure pile worms, although I doubt they actually knew where their next meal was coming from.

My study of worms has produced some interesting facts. I bet you didn't know that a worm has five hearts, or that there are 2,700 different kinds of earthworms. My source also says, "It's hard to imagine something more interesting to watch than an earthworm giving birth." I'll have to put that one on my list of Fun Things to Do in My Free Time.

In another publication I learned you can go out to the typical golf course putting green, drive a couple of metal stakes into the ground, connect wires between the stakes and the terminal to a car battery, and watch about 10,000 night crawlers come flying up out of the ground. Well, I'm not exactly sure of the number, but a lot of big worms, enough to keep you in bait for years, as long as you don't feed them coffee grounds. It is my impression that some industrious people actually gather worms in this manner and then sell them. If you're thinking of taking up the practice, however, I suggest you do it in the middle of the night. I don't know what the laws are in regard to the collection of worms from putting greens, so you're on your own. I think it might be embarrassing to be arrested for worm theft. If it turns out your jail mate is a bank robber and he asks, "What are you in for?" don't tell him.

Just recently I read a report in which researchers claimed that worms don't feel pain. In all my years of baiting hooks, I have felt twinges of guilt every time I threaded a worm on a hook. Now I find out they don't feel pain—*they've been faking it*!—just to play on my sense of guilt!

If you can't trust a worm, whom can you trust?

The very best worms for fishing, I determined years ago, are those that have been power-tilled in gardens. They're tough, angry, and belligerent, and perfect for catching wily fish of all kinds, particularly walleye and other arrogant species. Power tillers are expensive, of course, but well worth the price for tough, street-wise worm: "You wanna piece of me?" they growl at the fish. "You wanna rumble? Let's see what you got!"

The worms you buy at gas stations and other places of business are mostly raised on worm farms. They have grown up pampered and coddled and simply don't have the menacing personality of your power-tilled or even your manure-pile worms. One word of caution, though, should you ever buy commercial worms. If you go into a backwoods gas station and find a large, rough-looking woman behind the cash register, don't ask, "Do you have worms?" My friend Retch Sweeney did that a while back. He should get out of his full-body cast any day now. I'm exaggerating. The cast covers only part of his body. I won't mention which part.

I took the metal box from Bun and dropped it in my vest pocket.

"Perfect," I said. I guess she must be aware she's married to a scholar of worms. How great can that be!

Shaping Up for the Hunt

The exercise fad in this country is reaching epidemic proportions. You can't have a simple business meeting anymore without your associates comparing their tennis elbows, shin splints, charley horses, and athlete's feet. It's downright disgusting. Even my boss walked up to me the other day and asked if I would like to see his Adidas. I said, "What do you think I am, a pervert or something?" It turned out he was talking about his new pair of tennis shoes!

Exercise addicts are bad enough, but the pushers are worse. Everywhere I turn, somebody is trying to get me to take up jogging, bodybuilding, isometrics, yoga, kung fu, karate, or some other form of premeditated self-destruction. I tell them I'm an outdoorsman and just *being* an outdoorsman is adequate exercise.

Take, for example, my experience of loading a canoe on my car rack the other day. Knowing how even the slightest breeze can foil the success of this maneuver, I sacrificed one of my few remaining hairs to a test of wind velocity. The hair drifted quietly to the ground. Thus assured, I grabbed the canoe and, with a movement so smooth and graceful the vessel scarcely grazed my protruding eyeballs, snapped it straight up over my head.

At that instant, there arrived on the scene the strongest gust of wind recorded in our state in over half a century. The canoe sailed over the top of my wife's rose garden, mowed down a picket fence, ricocheted off a telephone pole, and turned end over end twice before starting to skitter across the street. At that point, and none too soon, I managed to release my grip on the thing and narrowly avoided being run over by the Avon lady.

My injuries were confined to an imaginative but tasteful reordering of my skeletal structure and a bad bruise on my leg where an unsuccessful attempt had been made to substitute a canoe thwart for a left femur. In those thirty seconds, I had enough exercise to last the average person for five years, but I can't seem to convince anyone of the fact. If you don't spend two hours a day running around in a sweatshirt, health addicts think you're either courting thrombosis or deliberately trying to antagonize the deodorant companies.

A while back I was slumped over the breakfast table performing my usual morning ritual of gluing my psyche back into some semblance of a human consciousness with caffeine, nicotine, cholesterol, and the headlines of the morning paper, when I happened to glance out the kitchen window and catch sight of my neighbor running down the alley in what appeared to be his pajamas. Now, Al Finley, a rather portly chap, is a member of the city council but is otherwise of good reputation. He usually conducts himself in a dignified and rational manner, so it was natural for me to assume that he was being pursued by someone, probably one or more of his dissatisfied constituents. While I was still pondering the vagaries of the political life, he ran by again, this time in the opposite direction.

By gosh, I said to myself, there must be more than one after him, because somebody obviously headed him off at the end of the alley and drove him back this way. After he made a couple more passes up and down the alley and was beginning to show signs of exhaustion, I decided to do what I could to save him from the mob. I stepped out on the back porch and yelled, "Jump the fence, Finley, and I'll hide you in the coal bin! I don't care what it is you've done." He gestured weakly at me in a manner I can describe only as unappreciative and kept on running.

"All right!" I shouted after him. "Let them get you. It'll serve you right!"

As I was walking by his house on my way to work an hour later, he emerged unscathed from his front door. He said he hoped he hadn't offended me by rejecting my offer of sanctuary. I said that it was all right, and you couldn't expect a person to be civil when he was running for his life.

"I wasn't running for my life," Finley replied. "I was jogging."

"Jogging? What on earth for?"

"I've already lost two inches around my waist," he said.

"I see," I said, deciding not to pursue the subject. It was clear the strain of fleecing taxpayers over the years had undermined his sanity, and I had no wish to nudge him further into the abyss. Nevertheless, he chose to explain.

"Have you forgotten hunting season is coming up in less than two months?" He gave me a look of having made everything clear. "You ought to do some jogging yourself."

"Look, Finley," I said gently. "I've hunted deer since I was twelve years old, and not once in all that time has a situation arisen requiring me to jog after them. Besides, the deer don't like it, and it makes the other hunters nervous."

He stared at me vacantly, then got in his car and drove off shaking his head. It was a sad spectacle to witness, even in a politician.

As if I hadn't had enough trouble already for one day, when I arrived at the office somewhat later than usual, my secretary was a picture of torment: legs and hands clamped together, teeth clenched, eyes bulging, face the color of an overripe pomegranate.

"Uh, sorry I'm so late, Midge," I said. "If you need to step out for a moment, I'll answer the phone."

"Whew!" she said, sagging into her chair. "I was just doing my daily isometrics."

"That was my impression," I said, "but I'd prefer you not do one in the office."

"Isometrics are an exercise for toning up the muscles!" she snapped.

Actually, I knew all about isometrics. I told Midge about the time my friend Retch Sweeney caught the exercise bug, and how, before he recovered his senses, it cost him a good deal of embarrassment and nearly his life. Once, when returning from a fishing trip, Retch stopped at a little roadside diner conspicuous for its total lack of other patrons. The steak he ordered and the price of it aroused in Retch the suspicion that the place was run by a combination of highwaymen and horse thieves.

After the main course and while waiting for his dessert, Retch decided to pass the time profitably by performing isometrics, an exercise he hoped would convey the impression that he was a physical fitness buff and could turn deadly should the gang attempt to rob him. As it turned out, the cook and the waitress had never heard of isometrics but were well practiced in the latest first-aid procedure for saving a person strangling on his dinner. The cook caught Retch in a crushing bear hug from behind, driving all the wind out of him with sufficient force to blow all the flies off a mound of hamburger ten feet away.

"Say your name!" the cook shouted, driving his balled fist into Retch's solar plexus. "Say your name!"

As soon as Retch recovered enough to speak, be blurted out, "Retch! Retch!"

"It ain't working," shouted the waitress. "He's still retching!"

By this time, the cook was using Retch's rib cage as an accordion, squeezing out, among other things, a tune Retch thought he recognized as either "Turkey in the Straw" or "The Battle Hymn of the Republic."

Just before the waitress made a last-ditch effort to reach down Retch's throat with a pair of spaghetti tongs, Retch managed to clear up the misunderstanding. The cook and the waitress had themselves a good laugh and as a gesture of goodwill allowed Retch to leave the premises without committing further assault on his person.

Although I generally question the veracity of Retch's stories, I told Midge that I thought this one was true. She said she didn't believe a word of it and that Retch and I had probably made it up, simply to poke fun at the new health fads. As a card-carrying health sadist herself, she took the opportunity to express her opinion that I could use a bit of exercise myself.

"Ha!" I said. "Hunting season is coming up. That is all the exercise I need."

"Yeah, right," she said. "Listen, you spend a lot of time running around in the woods all by yourself. Have you ever stopped to think what would happen if you suffered a fatal infarction way off in some wild place?"

Up until that point, I hadn't even realized infarctions could be serious, let alone fatal. Since Midge reads health magazines all the time, though, I figured she must know what she's talking about. With the acumen of a life-insurance salesman, she had succeeded in igniting in me some doubt about the length of my longevity. I sat around the rest of the morning, enveloped in a heavy gloom relieved by occasional twinges of fear. I thought about suffering a fatal infarction on my next hunting trip, and how my companions would grieve, sitting around the campfire talking about what a great guy I had been, and how out of respect to my remains perhaps they should cut the hunting trip short by a day or two, depending on the weather and if anyone had turned up some really fresh signs.

OK, I thought. So maybe it wouldn't hurt to do a bit of exercising to get ready for the hunt, even though it was a couple months away.

During my lunch hour, I slipped down to the public library and checked out an armload of books on various kinds of exercise. I asked the librarian if she had a book titled *The Drinking Man's Exercise.* I vaguely recalled having heard of such a book, and supposed that it would deal with such things as elbow bending, bellying up to the bar, and tossing down shots. She said she had never heard of it and wouldn't order it if she had. She did suggest an alternative, but I told her I was interested in improving my physique, not my character. I immediately discovered that reading exercise books can be dangerous to your health. Plowing through the first one, *Let's Put the Fit Back into Fitness*, I narrowly escaped being bored to death, and as it was, went about four days afterward with the distinct sensation of having my brain submerged in a tuna casserole. The one sound bit of information I managed to extract from the book was some advice to the effect of this: Before undertaking any program of strenuous exercise, one should obtain a physical from a medical doctor. I was in complete agreement with this suggestion. Doctors are by far the best people to get a physical from, if for no other reason than they don't laugh and poke fun at you when you take your clothes off. This is not to say that they are not above cracking a joke or two at your expense. While I was explaining to my own doctor that I was planning to undertake some serious exercise, I happened to mention that I thought I had lost quite a bit of weight since my last physical.

"You didn't lose it," he said. "It just slipped around to your rear where you can't see it." Personally, I think it is particularly bad for doctors to laugh at their own jokes and even more so in front of their naked patients. It tends to undermine one's confidence in the medical profession.

A physical from my doctor, old Fred, is such an ordeal that you need to get a physical to prepare you for the physical.

He tops it all off by hooking you up to an electrocardiograph machine and making you run on the treadmill. After a few minutes on the treadmill, I was dripping with sweat, gasping for breath, and buckling at the knees. I knew I couldn't last much longer.

"How am I doing?" I asked Fred.

"Not bad," he said. "Now let's try it with the treadmill turned on."

He revved up the machine to about thirty miles an hour. My legs instantly dissolved into molten lead, but I had to keep running to avoid being slurped down into the treadmill innards. All the while, old Doc Fred stood there munching on a doughnut and drinking a cup of coffee.

"I don't think you understand, Doc," I finally croaked. "I'm going to shoot a deer with a rifle, not run him down on foot and strangle him with my bare hands."

"Stop whining," he said kindly. "You're nearly finished."

"You're telling me," I gasped.

When the physical was completed, he fed all the information into a computer, which spewed out a stream of paper filled with a mass of graphs. Then he sat down to interpret the results for me.

"Oh, oh," he said frowning. "A&P Iron has dropped thirty points. I'd better schedule you for a couple of operations."

"What? What!" I exclaimed. "Does that mean I'm done for?"

"No, it means I am. This is a report from my stockbroker. Now let's take a look at *your* printout. Ah, I see you have some squiggles here in the cardiovascular section."

"Uh, are squiggles serious, Doc?"

"I've never had anyone die from squiggles, but we'd better keep an eye on them to make sure they don't develop into doodles. Actually, I have to say you are in excellent condition, even for a man twice your age."

"Great!" I said.

"Of course that doesn't mean you couldn't drop dead stepping over the cat."

"But I wanted to run up and down mountains, camp, hunt, fish!"

"That's all right," he said. "Just don't step over any cats."

After receiving a clean bill of health and another bill I interpreted as an attempt to recoup his stock market losses in one fell swoop, I immediately started shaping up for the impending hunting season.

The first exercise program I tried was from a book called, simply, *Yoga*. I chose it because yoga could be performed in the privacy of one's own home and didn't require making a public spectacle of one's self, as did, for example, jogging. Somehow Finley heard I had taken up exercising and kept glued to the window hoping to catch me in the act.

In my first yoga posture, I attempted something called the Lotus, from which posture I was finally able to extricate myself by snagging a cane from a corner next to the door and prying my legs apart. It was then that I perceived yoga would be an absolutely useless exercise when it came to shaping up for the hunt. No, there had to be something else. I quickly reviewed all my hunting experiences and immediately came up with the perfect exercise for hunters: standing still!

People who are not outdoor sportsmen don't realize how much time is spent standing still while hunting. Very often, a hunter will stand still behind a tree, while a mile away a deer also will choose to stand still. The first one to move loses. Brilliant! I immediately got up off the floor and stood still in front of the television for thirty minutes straight. It was exhausting, but one must do what one must do in order to shape up for the hunt.

A Bit about My Writing Life

I have just taken the measure of Mark Twain's auto-biography, the edition published in 2010. Despite small type, it is two and three-quarter inches thick. My own auto-biography, which I am starting at this moment, twenty minutes after two, the ninth of January, 2011, a snowy after-noon, will not be so thick. Its main advantage over Twain's is that it can be read in a matter of minutes as opposed to years. As with Twain, I will not let facts stand in the way of a good story, but for the most part will stick to the truth as I know it. In regard to pertinent events that occurred before I was born, all that would be hearsay. I cannot vouch for any of it. Much to my disappointment, my family apparently contained no known bandits, murderers, pirates, bank rob-bers, or even any common criminals.

Counting my own father, we did have a couple of war heroes. The other one was my great-grandfather, Archibald Hall, who fought for the North during the Civil War. One of the interesting things about him is that he was wounded during one of the many battles in which he was a participant. I was perhaps only six or seven when my grandmother told me about her father's getting wounded in the Civil War. Needless to say, I instantly became enormously proud of my great-grandfather. Later, however, Gram told me the wound consisted of getting one of his big toes shot off! This struck me right away as a suspicious wound. Think about it. There are the big toes, tramping along in the dirt and mud, and one Confederate soldier says to another, "Bart, I bet you can't shoot off one of that Yank's big toes." Well, it would be an impossible shot. Also, had I been in my great grandfather's shoes at that moment, with a whole army shooting at me, I can tell you my two big toes would have been moving very fast. They wouldn't be standing around just waiting to get shot off. Then there was the possibility that if you got a big toe shot off, you would be sent to the rear, to a hospital, or even all the way home. Getting a big toe shot off would be like having one of the Rebs do you a favor. Big toes aren't of that much use anyway. All my pride in that wound evaporated. A big toe! Years later, when I was doing some research on my ancestors, I discovered that my great-grandfather wasn't in the infantry but the cavalry! His big toe was way up there on the side of a horse and easy to pick off. Furthermore, I learned that Archibald Hall fought in nearly every major battle of the Civil War from beginning to end. He apparently wasn't someone to be bothered much by the loss of a big toe. Anybody named Archibald, of course, learns to be a fearless fighter early on.

My grandmother told these stories sitting in the dark by our old wood-burning stove whenever the electricity went off and the lights out, her rocking chair squeaking away as she created magical pictures in the dark.

During World War I, my father, Frank McManus, received a commendation from his commanding officer, Major Douglas MacArthur, chief of staff of the Rainbow Division during the war. The commendation was for defending a particular hill. When I was six, he died of cancer, which

I believe was the result of his having inhaled a dose of mustard gas during the war.

My mother, Mabel, was a country school teacher. She earned $75 a month teaching all eight grades, putting on plays for parents, Christmas parties for the pupils, cooking the hot lunch at noon and serving it, getting our drinking water out of a creek, hauling in the firewood, and keeping the old barrel stove going, its sides eaten through by heat and rust, but the holes putting on a wonderful light show across the ceiling during the dark of night.

This was at the old log school house far back in the woods near Priest Lake, Idaho. The two years we spent at that school pretty well shaped my approach to life. I ran free for two whole years, when I should have been in first and second grade. Mom never paid much attention to my education, her time and energy used up on the pupils she was paid to teach, so I was allowed to run wild along Goose Creek and in the surrounding woods and mountains whenever I wanted, which was most of the time. During winter, I went to sleep every night listening to wolves howl as they made their nightly hunt along the ridge above the school. "Send Pat out!" they seemed to be howling. "Send Pat out!"

Mom flunked me in second grade. I once heard her tell friends that her daughter, Patricia, six years my senior, was very smart, but Pat was "slow." Many years later, we came across my second grade report card in her papers. Under the part that said "Reason for Failure," she had written, "Too many absences." When you think about it, that is a remarkable achievement, for someone who lives at the school. As I say, those two years at the little log cabin school shaped all of my future life. From then on, my major goal was to achieve as much freedom as possible. Rich was OK, but I could live without it, as long as I was free.

Patricia eventually became widely known as "the Troll," one of the most popular characters in my humor pieces. I am happy to report she was immensely proud of the title, and sometimes received letters addressed only to "Troll."

At age seven, I taught myself to read. I pulled a third-grade reader off the shelf, climbed up on my bed, opened it to the first story, and told myself, "I'm not leaving this bed until I can read this story perfectly." I already knew phonics, from having been raised in country schoolrooms practically from the time I was born. I sounded my way through that story a dozen times. Eventually, I perceived that the story was about peanuts, mainly about how they were grown. It was the stupidest story I've ever read. The only interesting thing I learned from it was that peanuts are grown under the ground, not on top of it, as I had assumed. But from then on, I knew how to read.

At supper that evening, I told my mother, "I learned to read today."

She said, "That's nice. Pass the potatoes."

When we moved back to our little farm three miles north of Sandpoint, Idaho, I frequented the county library at least once a week. The librarian back then remains one of my heroes. Her name was Mary McKinnon. Mary directed me to all kinds of books over the years, including my days as a graduate student in college. She had put together a wonderful library on the second floor of Sandpoint's City Hall. For some unknown reason, I became fascinated with the Bobbsey Twins books when I was in third grade. Even now I can recall their names—Flossie and Freddie. (Or maybe Fanny and Fred? My memory isn't that good anymore.) No doubt Mary tried to direct me to more advanced reading, but I doubt she succeeded until I had read every last one of the Twins series, at least those about Flossie and Freddie. Looking back, I have not the slightest idea what so fascinated me about those two chubby little characters.

Early on in life, I decided to be an artist. In my mind, painting would give me the greatest degree of freedom. I would paint pictures and sell them, and then be free to do whatever else I wanted. When I reached college age, my high school art teacher told me that the art department at Washington State College was the best around. So I decided to go there, even though it was out of state and my tuition would be much higher than at the University of Idaho. Fortunately, I had made and saved quite a lot of money working for farmers the summer after my high school sophomore year, and construction the summers after my junior and senior years. One of my best jobs was as a high-scaler, where my crew of four hung by ropes over sheer cliffs and cleared them of loose rock. It was dangerous work—but the advantage was that if the foreman wanted to yell at you, he had to come down the side of a cliff on a rope to do it. Then one day a high-scaler on one of the crews got killed, and the superintendent decided that from then on no one under eighteen could work as a high-scaler. I was seventeen, and so lost the best job I've ever had. There is a great sense of freedom that comes from dangling over a cliff on a rope.

The following year, I enrolled at Washington State College as an art major, with the intent of becoming another Norman Rockwell. Alas, the WSC art faculty hated Norman Rockwell and his art, particularly his *Saturday Evening Post* covers. As a result, I was totally lost in regard to what direction I might pursue in terms of a future career. At the same time, I was not doing well in Freshman Composition. My instructor, one Milton Pederson, was tough! Every week, we comp students had to write a composition. After five or six weeks, I had received nothing but Ds and Fs.

Then one day, Milt said, "Look for the telling detail," and it was as if a bomb went off in my head. Suddenly I knew what writing was all about. My grades began to improve. Right away I had a major breakthrough: a D-plus! Then came a C-minus, followed by a whole C, and so on to the end of the quarter. On my last essay, Milt awarded me an A-plus and a recommendation for Honors English. My essay, by the way, was about Norman Rockwell. Scarcely had I learned what an irony was than I had committed one.

Many years later, I was at a dinner for a large number of people and Milt happened to be there, so I told the story about receiving an A-plus in his class. Milt roared out,

"I never gave an A-plus in my entire life!" But he had. And he had singlehandedly turned me into a writer.

By my sophomore year I was selling features to the *Lewiston Morning Tribune*. Although I would have a series of actual jobs for the next twenty-five years, my major drive was finally to make a living at freelance writing. This happened in the 1960s, although I would continue with actual employment for a few more years.

My stories in those early years were based on facts, requiring research and photography, but it was all exciting and wonderful. I wrote for two hours a night, seven nights a week. Perhaps the one distinguishing element in my factual stories is that I tried to include humor in each of them. Two of those stories are included in this collection: "Wild Life in a Room with a View," first published in *Sports Illustrated*, later abridged in *Reader's Digest*, and "There Goes the Indian with the Digital Wristwatch," published in *TV Guide*. Those two stories formed the pinnacle of my career as a factual freelance writer. I probably could have continued as a factual writer from then on, but a peculiar thing happened.

One night I finished an article in the first hour of my two-hour writing schedule. It was about the use of telemetry in the study of wildlife, hooking up assorted wild creatures with radio transmitters so scientists could study their movements at night. Because I stuck fiercely to my two-hour writing schedule, I decided to write a piece of nonsense to fill up my second hour. My head was already crammed with factual information about telemetry, so I decided to write a piece of nonsense about it, the comic idea being that eventually all wildlife would be hooked up with radio transmitters, which would simplify hunting immensely. I knocked off the piece of nonsense in an hour, stuck it in an envelope, sent it to *Field & Stream*, and forgot about it. I had a rule in those days that everything I wrote, no matter how bad I thought it was, I sent off to a magazine (a confession some critics have picked up on). Weeks passed. And then one day I went out to our mailbox and there was a small envelope from *Field & Stream*. My heart leaped. Writers place major importance on the size of envelopes they receive from publishers. Large envelopes contain the rejected manuscript; small envelope contain checks. This small envelope contained a check for $350. That may not seem like a lot of money, but it transformed me. Writing factual articles is hard, time-consuming work requiring much travel and research. A factual article I had just published had paid me $750, but I had spent weeks researching and writing it. Now here was a check for $350, payment for a piece of nonsense that had taken me an hour to write. I did some rapid calculations and was instantly transformed into a humor writer. Within a year, I had more markets than I could keep up with, and the rates of payment grew with every sale. Suddenly I had achieved the goal I had set for myself at that little log cabin school in the backwoods of Idaho—freedom! That freedom required that I work all the time, of course, but it was still freedom, and that freedom eventually took me all over the world, beyond anything I had ever imagined as a seven-year-old.

Along the way, I acquired a wife, Darlene, also known in my stories as "Bun." There is an essay in this collection that tells of my pursuit of her. I was still in high school when I met her, and she was already in college with a boyfriend in the service. The odds were heavily against me, but I've never been good at math and couldn't calculate them. Along the way, we accumulated a huge family: four daughters, five grandsons, four granddaughters, one great-grandson, and three great-granddaughters. The cost of college tuitions has curtailed my freedom considerably, but what's so great about freedom anyway? The family is terrific.

In the mid-1970s I packaged up thirty or so of my published humor pieces and started sending them around to book publishers. As usual, rejection letters started flowing in. Sometimes I would send the package to one publisher and get it back from another. Eventually, I would find out that the editor at the first publisher had really liked the stories and wanted to do a book, but the marketing department had turned it down. The marketing department! And here I thought editors were in charge. The first editor would then send the manuscript to a friend of his at another publisher and that editor would return the manuscript to me, usually with a note saying he really liked it but the marketing department . . .

After several months of rejections, I was offered a teaching job at a university in Guadalajara, Mexico. We packed up the kids and left. The very day after we had a phone installed in our Guadalajara apartment, I got a phone call from two different publishers wanting the book. I took the first one to call, naturally. An hour after the second call, I got a call from an agent wanting to represent me. Someone at the publishers had called him about me. Publishers prefer to work with agents rather than writers, I don't know why. So you see, everything works backward in the publishing world. I think the two books I'm working on now will bring my total to twenty-five, but I'm too old and tired to get up and count them.

And that, in a nutshell, is how I became a writer.

Big

Perhaps the most overused word in the vocabulary of outdoorsmen is *big*. For example, when you ask how a fishing trip went, the angler replies, "Oh, I caught several small ones, but mostly they were big." The listener must evaluate this information. "Big," in this context, depends on the size of the small ones. If the small ones were six-inchers, the *big* ones may only have been ten-inchers, scarcely what we would normally refer to as *big* fish. I point this out not in the way of criticism but in the interest of precision. On the other hand, I would not wish to deprive any fisherman of his use of the vague. A reputation often depends on it, and I certainly don't intend to put the reputation of any outdoorsman in jeopardy. What else do we have?

The use of *big* in reference to any outdoor activity—other than fishing, of course—can actually be dangerous. I remember as a youngster camping out with friends one time on Schweitzer Creek. It was a tiny stream tumbling out of a narrow mountain canyon a couple miles from where we lived. An hour's hike up the canyon took us to one of the world's greatest camping spots. Any kid who grows up without knowing such a campsite is seriously deprived. If I had time, I would get a certain congressman I know to pass a law against such an occurrence. (He no doubt would undertake this chore for me, but I don't know if he has been released yet.)

The unique feature of this campsite was that it required no tent. Sometimes we took a tent anyway, but only because we wanted to. (What's the point of having a tent if you don't use it?) The reason a tent wasn't required was because a high cliff rose up from the ground and slanted out over half or more of the rocky beach on which we camped. If it rained—there was something about our camping trips that triggered rain—we could build our campfire under the cliff, cook and eat our meals there, and spread out our sleeping bags to sleep while staying dry.

The little stream tumbled by the edge of the beach, and for a while at least, we could catch our breakfast right out of the pool that had been formed and stocked with fish perhaps a thousand years ago just for our benefit. An endless supply of firewood lay right at the edge of our camp. It was not quite under the cliff, so sometimes we had to put up with the discomfort of getting damp in the rain while we chopped a day's supply of firewood from a *big* cedar tree that had fallen across the creek. In the ten years or so that we camped at the site, our gathering of firewood did not make a dent in the tree. The last time I saw it, the cedar looked as if it had been gnawed on by a discriminating beaver and then abandoned.

Now, what was I writing about? Oh, yes, *big*. I did mention a *big* cedar, but, of course, you have no idea how *big* the big cedar was. If I said the cedar was as wide as a sidewalk and that you could cross to the other side of the creek on it without being scared of falling in, you would perhaps grasp the concept of "*big*"—in this case, at least. So here we had not only an infinite supply of firewood, but easy access to the other side of the creek provided by a single tree. What more could you ask of *big*?

One extremely dark night—actually, because of the depth and narrowness of the canyon, all of the nights were extremely dark—my friends and I suddenly heard an enormous racket over by the *big* cedar.

"What is it?" I whispered to Norm.

"I don't know," he whispered back. "But it's *big*!"

Vern nudged me in the back. "Can Norm see what's making that racket?"

"I think so," I whispered to him. "He says it's *big*!"

Kenny nudged Vern. "What's making that racket?"

"Norm says it's *big*!"

"*Big*? It's gotta be a bear!"

Vern nudged me. "Kenny says it's a bear!"

"Cripes," I said. I nudged Norm. "It's a bear!"

"Oh, no!" he hissed, which is an expression that is hard to hiss—unless, of course, you have a *big* bear ten feet away from you.

It was a matter of considerable comfort to me that I had Norm between me and the bear. Norm, at the time, was a little fat kid and, I suspected, would provide the bear with a rather tasty hors d'oeuvre. By the time the bear was done snacking on Norm, I could be at the tiptop of the nearest pine.

Suddenly, the racket stopped. This could be a bad sign! Fortunately, for the rest of the night, not a single sound came from the *big* cedar. All four of us could attest to that, because none of us got any more sleep.

The next morning, we discovered that the racket had been made by a chipmunk gnawing his way into and through a bag of potato chips. Not only did one of the smallest of woodland creatures deprive us of a night's sleep, but he also ate one of our basic camp foods! You lose your potato chips on an outing, and you're as good as done for. It was a lucky thing for that chipmunk that he didn't show his smug face around our camp again. He would have been in *big* trouble!

I went to elementary and high school in a tough little logging town. Although it has been some time since I was in first or second grade, I can still recall the dreaded cry issued by one of my small compatriots: "Watch out! Here come the *big* kids!" This warning probably referred only to those male pupils in the fourth or fifth grades, who themselves were probably not all that *big*. Well, some of them were *big*. In those years, you didn't get past fourth grade until you could read, spell, and do fractions. I remember one kid—I'll call him Jethrow—who had been in fourth grade for at least three years. There were rumors that he was already shaving and perhaps dating the teacher, but I doubt they were true. He wasn't her type. But occasionally there was a really *big* kid in fourth or fifth grade. In any case, whenever the *"big* kid" alarm was sounded, we would take off, running for our lives. It was scary. Looking back, I don't recall any of us little kids ever being caught and tormented by a *big* kid. They were simply satisfied to take over the swings, slides, and merry-go-rounds we had so summarily abandoned. Nevertheless, such was the effect on me that the shout, "Here come the *big* kids!" still makes me cast sharp looks in all directions. You never know.

A conservative friend of mine was outraged recently—actually, he is more or less in a continuous state of outrage—by government laws that protect the wimps from the strong. He quoted Winston Churchill as saying, "If we have laws protecting the wimps from bullies, we will end up a nation of wimps!" When I was six or seven years old, I certainly would have supported any law that stated: "Big kids are no longer allowed to torment little kids." But when my conservative friend raised his objection to such a law, I myself, now an adult, was outraged. I'm a big fan of Churchill and can't imagine him ever using the word "wimps."

I asked my friend if, whether during his early years in school, he had ever been alarmed by the cry, "Here come the *big* kids!"

"Of course not," he said. "I was one of the *big* kids!"

I can still recall one of my four daughters, as a child, hopping about and yelling, "You took the *big* half!" As a college

English professor at the time, I had worked tirelessly to correct the girls' errors of speech. "There is no such thing as a *big* half," I'd point out. "A half is a half. You might, for example, have said, 'You took the bigger piece.'"

"OK, then, you took the bigger piece! How about that?"

"That's much better," I'd say. "But I deserve the bigger piece because I'm so much bigger."

$7,000 TV Historical Extravaganza

As any TV executive will tell you, $7,000 doesn't go very far toward producing a historical extravaganza. Take, for example, the experience of the special events people at KHQ-TV in Spokane, Washington, who produced *Trailblazers*, a bicentennial series based on regional history.

After they had rounded up their actors and 150 extras; provided horses, costumes, and authentic weapons; built sets; and put on a couple of full-scale battles, there was scarcely enough money left over to buy beer for the cast.

Producer Ivan Munk, known among the cast as "Cecil B. De Munk," admits that some of the money probably wasn't spent to the best advantage. "That's one of the problems with inexperience," he says. "But with what we know now, we could probably put on *Gone with the Wind* for a couple thousand."

The six-part series dramatizes the building of the Mullan Road over the Rocky Mountains; a Jesuit missionary's work with the Indians in the early 1800s; the struggles of a crippled grandmother and her seventy-seven-year-old brother-in-law making their way alone to Oregon in the winter of 1846; the defeat of a company of U.S. calvary by the allied Indian tribes of the Spokane area; the founding and colorful history of Spokane (done as a monologue); and the last major battle between the Indians and the Army in Washington Territory. The actors were mostly from amateur theatrical groups, chiefly volunteers. Extras included businessmen, ranchers, teachers, students, housewives, children, old people, and, for all anyone knows, maybe a few actual Indians.

So far, *Trailblazers* has been shown only on KHQ, but other stations around the country have expressed an interest in seeing the series, possibly with the idea of using it as a model for their own low-budget historical productions.

When word was put out that KHQ would be producing *Trailblazers*, a Spokane utilities company put up $7,000 for production costs, and many people donated services, skills, and props. Horse owners supplied horses, including feed and transportation. Gun clubs provided muzzleloaders. Women from the nearby town of Rosalia sewed costumes, and the men built a workable cannon, using wagon wheels and a length of sewer pipe. A church and a rancher each donated a covered wagon, and the Eastern Washington State Historical Society came through with a couple of tepees.

The KHQ staff was flabbergasted by the response. "I couldn't believe it," says Munk. "We had horses worth more than our whole budget for the series!"

The enthusiasm of the volunteer performers provided a few problems. In one scene, one hundred war-painted "Indians" were mixing it up with the cavalry. Leading the attack, through rifle and cannon fire, through billowing clouds of dust and gun smoke, was a beautiful Indian princess.

"Cut! Cut!" screamed director Jim Johns. "What's the beautiful Indian princess doing leading the attack?" Upon learning she had merely been carried away by the excitement of it all, Johns turned philosophical. "Oh, what the hell," he said.

According to Johns, one of the secrets of producing shoestring historical extravaganzas for TV is to say, "Oh, what the hell," almost as often as "Cut! Cut!"

Whenever possible, the re-enactments were staged at the original sites. With the help of volunteer historians, museum curators, and archivists, great care was taken to make each show accurate in historical detail. But the twentieth century kept showing up in cameo appearances. Shooting was constantly interrupted by jets, helicopters, and other aircraft. The Indian chief would show up wearing a digital wristwatch. The brave slithering through the grass with a knife in his teeth would be wearing sunglasses. When the Indians ran out to taunt the soldiers, there would be a strange kid in jeans and a white T-shirt hurling insults of his own. And every so often the camera would pan past a barbed-wire fence. "Oh, what the hell," Johns would say.

For authenticity, it had been decided to darken the white actors with body paint when they were to play the part of Indians. Producer Munk (who prefers the title "Chief Instigator") came up with the idea of applying the body paint with a spray gun. He envisioned walking down a row of extras and painting them like a picket fence. But the paint kept clogging the gun, and the idea had to be scrapped in favor of white Indians.

Aside from white Indians wearing wristwatches, sunglasses, and T-shirts, the extras turned in some remarkable performances. In one scene, a young man was so delighted with his part as a trooper that he grinned continuously, even when he was in deadly hand-to-hand combat with an Indian brave. As for the brave, he had fallen wounded, blood streaming from his side.

"Hey, where did you get the ketchup?" a fellow actor asked, envious of the realism.

"Get out of here!" the brave muttered. "You're ruining my best scene!"

It turned out that the red stuff wasn't ketchup at all. The brave had somehow stabbed himself with his own lance.

Another bit of nice realism was added by the chilling yells of an "Indian," as he and a trooper slid down a pine-clad slope, the Indian on the bottom. Upon being complimented on his performance, the Indian explained, "Performance nothing! Sliding over pine cones in your naked skin is murder."

Even the production crew could be counted on to mess up a few shots. At one point, Chief Instigator Munk got in KHQ's pickup truck and drove down the road to keep sightseers out of the scene. As the wagon train struggled past the camera, there, bouncing along in the background in pursuit of some relatively unobtrusive spectators, was the pickup, with the station's call letters emblazoned on its side.

Experienced production companies use only "empty" horses for westerns, but the *Trailblazers'* gang did not. There wasn't enough time and, according to Munk, besides "nobody knew how to empty them." The frequent indiscretions of horses ruined many a take, but leading actress Joan Welch managed to save one shot. She blocked the offending part of the horse from view with an ad-lib sweep of her cloak.

"Now that is what I call an improvisation," said Johns.

Mrs. Welch, a professor at a Spokane college, is not fond of horses. When her part required that she ride one, she overcame her fear sufficiently to sit on one with the understanding that the horse was to remain stationary. But someone had forgotten to tell that to the horse, which galloped off over the horizon, taking Mrs. Welch with him. Her "Whoas!" over her remote mic gradually faded into ominous silence.

"We were terribly worried," Johns recalls, "about whether she would make it back in time for us to finish shooting the scene. Luckily, it took her only half an hour to walk back."

To economize, the series was shot with only one camera. As a result, many scenes had to be performed repeatedly to achieve a variety of camera angles. The Indian encampment and the wagon train provided their own special camera problems, Johns says. "When your Indian encampment has only two teepees and your wagon train only two wagons, you have to choose your shots pretty carefully. And they're all close-ups."

To create the impression of a long wagon train, Johns would have a pioneer man and woman drive a wagon by in front of a teepee. Once the wagon had passed out of the frame, the camera would be shut off, the wagon would circle around, a different pioneer man and woman would climb up on the driver's seat, the camera would be turned on and "another" unit of the wagon train would pass by. And so on, until the impression of a wagon train was completed.

Munk said one of the things that amazed him the most about the series was how well the cast got along. "We have 200 people on location for sixteen-hour days, and I don't think there was a single argument."

The station has been flooded with letters praising the series, including one from Governor Thomas Judge of Montana, who said his state is interested in using *Trailblazers* as an educational and research tool.

But even beyond the public impact of the series, the project will remain a warm personal experience for those who participated in it. Larry Gants, a KHQ staffer who played a colonel in one of the military episodes, says, "My cavalry company actually developed an esprit de corps in a single weekend. When we were leaving to go home, nearly every man walked over and solemnly shook my hand, just as if they were being mustered out after a long and hard campaign. Damned if I didn't feel the same way myself."

Wild Life in a Room with a View

E ach June, about the time most people think of vacations and many begin moving to the seashore, a few hundred strangely assorted Americans head for the high mountains and great forests of the land. Their stated purpose is to help prevent forest fires. But what they really have in mind is the ultimate get-away-from-it-all, an escape into the blissful solitude of a delightful little wilderness penthouse—a U.S. Forest Service lookout station. Helping prevent forest fires is merely the price they must pay for their room with a view. Early each September, out they come again, and from their stories one wonders if the solitude is all that blissful, the price that mere, or the penthouse that delightful; there are, it seems, a few trials and even some tribulations.

To begin with, the living quarters are cramped—twelve to fourteen feet square—and are nestled atop towers anywhere from ten to one hundred feet high. Fuel, food, water, and all other supplies needed to sustain an easy life must be toted by hand up the stairs, which can seem interminable.

The sanitary facility is fifty yards off in the bushes, and the nearest source of water may be a mile or more down the mountain. During storms the higher towers have a tendency to sway sickeningly, lightning strikes with unmonotonous regularity a few feet from where the lookout is sitting (or kneeling), and balls of weird blue "fire" from time to time sizzle about the place like water on a hot skillet. The lookout is assaulted by insects, besieged by beasts, seared by the sun, chased by forest fires, and, perhaps worst of all, tortured incessantly by the monstrous silence. This is to say nothing of the work, but, as one lookout suggests, the work consists largely of being there.

The experience of the Forest Service suggests that no particular kind of individual is ideally suited to life in a tower suite, and the recruits who show up for training early each summer prove to be a strangely mixed lot: prim lady schoolteachers, college professors, ministers' wives, loggers, vacationing businessmen, farmers, grandmothers, coeds, honeymooners, old marrieds, beauty queens, students, female truck drivers, ex-marines, and cookie-baking housewives; in short, just about anyone who can shake off the fetters of routine life for three months.

Newlyweds long ago discovered that lookout towers make private places for honeymoons, and each forest usually has at least one couple launching its marriage atop a peak. Rangers, reluctant marriage counselors that they are, generally avoid pointing out to couples that if a marriage can survive a summer in a lookout tower, it can survive almost anything. Their fervent hope is that the rocks the marriage may be headed for aren't those at the foot of the tower. Familiarity may or may not breed contempt, but there is no doubt that the tiny cabins breed profuse amounts of familiarity. Paul Wilson, dispatcher for the Coeur d'Alene (Idaho) National Forest, recalls one couple that stopped speaking to each other fifteen minutes after being moved into their cabin. "Right then, I knew it was going to be a long, hard season," says Paul. "And it was, for all concerned."

But whatever small apprehensions the honeymooners may create for the rangers, newlyweds almost always turn out to be highly competent and dedicated fire lookouts, not to mention a source of considerable humor. Visitors to one of those bridal towers listened in fascination recently as a blue-jeaned bride gave her impressions about honeymooning on a lookout platform. "One thing I've noticed is that the days seem so long and the nights so short!" Her stricken husband hastened to explain that this was because the tower was the highest point in the mountains and was, consequently, the first thing the sun's rays touched in the morning and the last in the evening. The nights actually were shorter.

The Forest Service likes to man its towers with married couples whenever possible. For one thing, the lookouts are not so lonely; they can break the monotony by making either love or war. For another, the government gets two pairs of eyes for the price of one. The husband is paid for the five weekdays and the wife for Saturday and Sunday. In practice, of course, the husband and wife are both in the tower most of the time. As one official points out, "There just isn't that much else to do."

Sometimes the lookouts are single women. Last summer, twenty-three of the 233 stations in the Northern Region were operated by female fire spotters. The consensus among rangers is that they do an excellent job, frequently surpassing the men. "They are more observant," says a ranger. "They hold their interest well in what can be a monotonous job, and they keep meticulous records. They also keep their quarters in much better condition." One girl, a coed from Idaho State University, "who didn't know a meadow bottom from a ridge top," was assigned to an observation cab atop a 100-foot steel tower overlooking a vast area of the Nez Perce Idaho National Forest. Not only did she adapt quickly and well to this awesome place of work, but within two weeks she had memorized the names of every ridge and water drainage in sight. Other women operate the complex network of stations that serve as the communications center for the Forest Service and various other state and federal agencies.

Although men are preferred in stations where smoke chasing and fire fighting may be part of the duties, the Lava Butte station in the Deschutes National Forest in Oregon was once manned by a lady who did all her own fire fighting. Having formerly worked on a tugboat, she was known, naturally, as "Tugboat Annie." She further endeared herself to the foresters by smoking cigarettes in a long, elegant holder, which she would use to point out various features of the landscape to the occasional visitors.

Many of the women returned year after year. Mrs. Carol Sopher, the only woman lookout in the Bitterroot National Forest of Montana last year, has spent seventeen summers in fire towers, and Dorothy Taylor, a former schoolteacher, has worked for nearly twenty years in Montana's Lolo National Forest.

Not only are the rangers pleased to see the ladies return, but so are the squirrels and chipmunks that live in the rocks around the stations, for they receive a lot of maternal care. One lady fire watcher baked sugar cookies every day to feed to the golden-mantled squirrels around her station, and by summer's end she could bring them running by calling, "Here, kitty, kitty, kitty!" Another lady lookout fed her chipmunks hotcakes daily. "By the end of summer," says a ranger, "they were so fat they looked like marmots."

Larger wild animals, although seldom dangerous, contribute their full share to the tribulations of lookouts. Porcupines are fond of the salt in rubber and will eat the tires, and even the fan belts, off a lookout's automobile. Mountain goats like to gather in the middle of the night for a playful romp on the catwalk that surrounds the lookout's sleeping quarters. The goats so successfully upset the night of one lookout that he kept falling asleep during working hours, an offense that the Forest Service ranks about equal to that of the Army sentry who dozes at his post. He finally built a barricade to keep the goats off the tower stairs.

Many of the lookouts are from large cities and at first have some difficulty identifying their wild animals. A lookout once radioed that he had a coyote hanging around his tower. For several days, he entertained the boys back at the ranger station with descriptions of the antics of this friendly and daring animal. When he told one day of the coyote trying to claw its way into the cabin, the rangers decided they had better have a look at the critter. It turned out to be a bear. Another lookout, obviously nervous, reported, "Big, hairy beasts are ganging up around the foot of my tower." He went outside for another look, and quickly returned to the radio. "Now they're coming up the stairs!" he shouted. The local ranger leaped into his four-wheel-drive and flailed it all the way to the tower, his imagination conjuring up the wildest of Alfred Hitchcock scenes. The troublemakers turned out to be a family of pack rats.

Most of the lookouts develop their own methods for dealing with animals that make nuisances of themselves, as did the lady who observed a large bear ascending her tower stairs. When the bear did not heed her vocal threats, she went inside, heated a pot of water, and dumped it on him. He was not seen in the neighborhood again. This procedure, though it may seem absurdly domestic and urban, is now the approved procedure for discouraging bears that like to climb towers.

Occasionally, a bear will threaten a lookout with bodily harm, but only when the lookout is accompanied by a loyal and courageous dog and armed with much good advice is he likely to be in danger. Doug McFarland, a young lookout in the Primitive Area of idaho, was clearing a trail during one wet period when the fire danger was low. He was accompanied by his trusty Irish setter and had been told that if he saw a large bear preparing to mount an attack the best thing to do was to give a loud whoop. A couple of miles down the trail from his tower, McFarland noticed the first sign of a bear: the silent, reddish blur of his dog passing him, fleeing in the opposite direction. Shortly thereafter, the bear emerged from the brush, cleared the field for battle by ushering her twin cubs up a tree and charged. Quickly recalling the good advice, McFarland let out a loud whoop. The bear rushed on. McFarland whooped again. Still, the bear didn't stop. "My third whoop was entirely involuntary," McFarland recalls, "but apparently I at last had whooped authentically." The bear skidded to a stop a few feet away and returned reluctantly to her cubs. Shakily, McFarland made his way back to the lookout tower, where his dog awaited him under the bed.

There are other fire-watching hazards. The safest place to be during a lightning storm, rangers like to explain as they sit comfortably in their office swivel chairs, is a look-out tower. This, they claim, is because the towers are deco-rated with such a formidable mass of lightning rods that it is virtually impossible to be electrocuted there (rangers do not entertain the possibility of a person's being frightened to death). When lightning does strike a tower, the lookout is, of course, sitting at the point of impact. To fully appreciate the stimulating effect of this, you must recall the last time you saw a great ragged bolt of lightning split the sky and counted—1,001, 1,002 . . . until the sound of thunder finally arrived. In a lookout tower struck by lightning, the thunder and flash are simultaneous, creating an effect that is presum-ably like that of sitting inside an exploding bomb.

The rangers consider the first lightning storm as the qualifying exam for their new lookouts. "Up to then, they're amateurs," says one forester. "After it, they're pros." Last summer a new lookout became a pro his first night on the job. His tower was struck nine times. Asked if he would like a few days off to pull himself together, the lookout said no, he would stick to his post—an obvious case of shell shock.

In addition to lightning rods, the Forest Service sup-plies the lookout with a chair that has a glass insulator on the bottom of each leg. If the lookout sits in the chair, first making sure that it is not situated between two pieces of metal—electricity might arc between them—and if he avoids touching the radio or telephone, puts in his earplugs, and does not leap off the tower, he has an excellent chance of surviving strike after strike with nothing more serious than jangling nerves, psychedelic eyeballs, and recurrent nightmares.

Less spectacular than lightning but much more haunting are the weird balls of blue fire that sometimes are seen dancing about the lookout stations during electrical storms. This phenomenon is called St. Elmo's fire and is caused by harmless static electricity.

Forest fires seldom endanger lookouts, and if a fire should threaten a station there usually is ample time to beat a retreat. But not always. The Sundance Fire in Idaho in the summer of 1967 proved an exception for eighteen-year-old Randy Langston. Stationed on a 7,264-foot Roman Nose Peak, Randy had been keeping an eye on the fire, which had been burning fitfully for several weeks. On the evening of September 1, the fire was about fifteen miles and a mountain range away from the Roman Nose lookout. Then, in a matter of hours, a 60 mph wind whipped the Sundance blaze into one of the worst fires in Idaho's smoky history. In a single day, the fire made a run of twenty-one miles, eventually threatening towns, farms, and homes along a thirty-mile front. At its worst, it burned one square mile of mature timber every three minutes, and its smoke column rose to a height of 45,000 feet. Trapped in the middle of this inferno, Randy continued to make his radio reports until it became evident that the fire was going to sweep right over his tower. He was ordered to take his radio and try to find shelter in the rocks below the station. The young lookout scrambled down to a rock slide, where he spent the night surrounded by a violent fire storm. The following morning, a helicopter picked him up and flew him to safety. He was a bit shaken, but unsinged.

And the lookout tower? Well, it survived, too. It stands now as a lonely and useless sentinel over 51,000 charred acres that made up one of the most beautiful forest areas in Idaho.

The lookout begins his summer of tranquility by attending a week-long fireguard training school conducted by each national forest. There he learns the various methods of spotting and fighting fires. After completing his training, he usually moves straight into the lookout station he has been assigned to. Most of the stations now have roads leading to them, but a few can only be reached by a horse, helicopter, or on foot. In the early days of lookout stations, the lookout went in and stayed "in" for the season, but now he can usually have a day or two in town each week while a substitute takes his place. In the case of a married couple, the wife can hop in the car and drive to town for a loaf of bread or a divorce.

The first weeks at the station may be spent clearing trails, stringing telephone wires, maintaining roads, or giving the tower a new coat of paint. Daily weather reports are also made. Once the fire season arrives, however, which is usually in early June, lookouts concentrate on their primary job and every twenty minutes must make a systematic check of the area protected by their station. After a week or so, the twenty-minute check is all but forgotten, because the lookout is in the habit of looking. Indeed, he can hardly stop looking.

"After a while, they just look around all the time," a ranger explains. "You can't hold a decent conversation with them because their heads are constantly turning this way and that. They look like owls."

Competition between lookouts becomes fierce. Not only do they check their own territory but each other's, and it is a major triumph to spot an unreported "smoke" in the other fellow's range. Working hours as such become purely academic, and lookouts will make a habit of getting up in the middle of the night to make sure a fire hasn't sneaked into their area under cover of darkness. Needless to say, the Forest Service subtly encourages this spirit of friendly competition.

New lookouts at first have some trouble identifying smokes. They will report patches of fog, clouds, dust, and, at night, even the lights from each other's stations. But by the time fire season arrives, they have become experienced enough to know smoke when they see it. Still, they tend to be jumpy and don't take any chances. Last summer during the height of the Idaho fire season, a lookout reported smoke he had just spotted. As it happened, a plane loaded with retardant to be dumped on another fire was just clearing the runway. It was ordered to the new blaze instead. Fortunately, the pilots are required to make a dry run over each suspected site before they bomb. Down below, the pilot could see a logging crew staring nervously up at him as he roared over at treetop level. The smoke was a plume of blue exhaust fumes caused by starting a bulldozer.

Base pay for lookouts ranges from $2.15 to $2.40 an hour. They also may earn a monthly increment from 15 percent to 25 percent of their base pay by working an additional twenty-eight hours a week. They must furnish all of their own provisions, but the room—and the view—is free.

In recent years most of the stations have been "modernized," which means that wood-burning stoves have been replaced with propane combination stove-refrigerator units. If the lookout's stove burns wood, he must split it himself, regulations requiring that he keep a two-week supply on hand at all times. Stations unequipped with propane also have no means of refrigeration, thus depriving the lookout of the luxury of perishable foods and cool drinks (one young lookout's parents eased—or perhaps ruined—their son's summer on his own by flying their private plane over his station every couple of days and parachuting him a quart of ice cream.) The only time any of the lookouts have running water is if they should break into a sprint while carrying it in a bucket up from the nearest spring.

The Forest Service is quite concerned that its lookouts not go overboard with the "roughing it" concept. The lookouts are representatives of the U.S. government, the rangers point out, and are expected to create a favorable impression. There is no telling when one of the taxpayers may show up for an impromptu visit, regardless of where the station is located, and he is not to find empty food cans moldering on the floor or shorts and bra hung up to dry on the firefinder. After each sprinkling of rain, the windows—all forty or so panes—are to be polished spotlessly clean. Ledges must be dusted daily and the floors and steps—no matter how many of them—must be swept. The grounds are to be kept free of clutter by burning or burying debris.

Lookout stations, once merely functional, are now becoming tourist attractions of sorts. They make excellent destinations for hiking clubs. If he gets careless, a lookout who has not seen another human in a month could find himself kicking cans under his bunk, dusting the table with the T-shirt he has just snatched from the firefinder, and setting his abode in acceptable U.S. representative-type order as thirty-seven members of the Hill Hoppers Outing Club ascend his stairs. The government is even publishing little pamphlets describing lookout stations that the public might like to visit.

The Forest Service currently operates approximately 1,000 lookout stations throughout the country during the fire season. The number has decreased by several hundred during the last few years as many areas changed from detection systems relying almost entirely on fixed ground lookouts to ones employing a few key ground stations supplemented by aircraft patrol. But there is no thought that the ground stations can ever be completely abandoned. Thus, he who would escape for three whole months the grit and grind of people-glutted cities to spend the summer on a Forest Service lookout station will have the opportunity. There is no need to rush. Simply obtain from your local post office and fill out several copies of the Application for Federal Employment, Standard Form 57, and mail them to the ranger district in the national forest of your choice. The Forest Service usually hires its lookouts during January, but a few replacements are taken on as late as May.

So just imagine it. There you are, relaxing on the tower steps as the sun sinks slowly in the west and the darkness rises out of the pine-clad depths of the mountains, finally to embrace this little penthouse, your room with a view. Touched by the last lingering rays of the sun, the tower glows like the first star of evening in the great blue bowl of the sky. Peace. Beauty. Somewhere off down the mountain, a coyote wails. Then your keen, woodsman-type ear picks up a faint sound. It is the sound of porcupines gnawing the tires off your car. From the edge of an alpine grove, you glimpse a herd of mountain goats approaching your tower stairs. The breeze is picking up, the tower is beginning to sway, and rising in the south, blotting out the stars, is a massive thunderhead. It is times like this that you truly rejoice in your solitude; there is no one around to hear you cry.

Risk Assessment

Help! I'm being held captive in a canoe by the most boring person in the entire history of the world!

Allow me to point out something you already know, and that is that a canoe is a vehicle of very close confinement. Furthermore, if you are on a ten-day canoe trip, you are not likely ever to arrive at a point along the way where you can simply get out and walk home. This is particularly true if the canoe belongs to you.

If someone bores you on the phone, you can always shout out something like, "Good heavens, the house is on fire! Got to go!" In a canoe, you have no such choice. I suppose you could shout out, "Jump, the canoe is on fire!" then paddle away as soon as your companion was overboard. But it's way too easy to tell a canoe isn't on fire. No, you must sit there day after day and listen to the endless prattle of your fellow canoeist. "Prattle," by the way, is to raise your partner's level of conversation by an astronomical degree. "Duh" would be a response from him comparable to Archimedes' cry of "Eureka!"

"Wow!" you say to your canoe partner. "Look at that sunset!"

"Duh!"

But I have no one to blame but myself. I had failed to run a risk assessment on my potential canoe partner. He was a college professor. That in itself should have set off alarm bells, but I failed to detect any. A proper risk assessment can save you endless difficulties in the selection of companions for hunting, fishing, camping, and canoeing.

Often, though, we will do a risk assessment and then fail to apply it to the appropriate situation. A friend of mine recently told me about a fellow with whom he and some of his other pals hunted. On three separate hunting trips, my friend told me, this fellow's rifle went off accidentally, once in the car, once as he was getting out of the car, and once in the hunting cabin. As a result of my interest in risk assessment, I started to ask my friend a question.

"Stop!" he cried, raising his hands. "I know! I know! I know what you're going to ask. After the first accidental discharge, why did we continue hunting with the guy?"

"It seems to call for a risk assessment."

"He owned the hunting cabin!"

"Oh, right! A hunting cabin is well worth the risk. Excuse me for even questioning your motive."

Obviously, my friend in this instance had made an assessment and concluded a hunting cabin was well worth the risk. That is my point exactly. Risks are often highly rewarding, particularly if you survive. But make sure you weigh them carefully beforehand. Risks are not brussels sprouts after all. Actually, brussels sprouts are not without risk, but I don't want to go into that.

Here's a perfect example of what can happen if you don't weigh risks before undertaking a venture. Kenny, Norm, Vern, and I, my hunting, fishing, and camping companions, were returning from a camping trip high in the mountains. We were all about sixteen. Having been out for a week, and having climbed five mountain peaks that demanded climbing, we were all exhausted. We decided to take a short-cut on our way out of the mountains. The shortcut had hardly started when we came to a high mountain blocking our way—Beehive. The mountain had overlapping layers of rock that resembled the sides of a wild beehive.

We now had two choices. We could climb up over the top of Beehive in relative safety, or we could drop down through thick woods and brush to the river far below and go around it. And I discovered a third choice. I noticed a narrow rock ledge running around the steep side of the mountain right on our level. It was directly ahead of us. If we worked our way around Beehive on the ledge, we wouldn't have to climb either up or down. Brilliant! But what if, as we worked our way around Beehive, the ledge started to peter out and even-tually disappeared altogether! This was the risk I failed to assess. Halfway around, the ledge began to narrow. Before long, we were leaning into the rock, our boots turned side-ways on the ledge and overlapping its outer edge by inches. For some reason I've forgotten, we could not turn around and go back. I think it had something to do with having to hop in the air, turn our feet around, and hope we landed back on the narrow ledge when we came down. There was also the problem that each of us carried a heavy pack, which seemed to be pulling us out into empty space. Far down below, we could see the tops of tall pines, the tips of which seemed to be beckoning to us with long green fingers. At this point the group's confidence in me as a leader seemed to diminish. And then, suddenly, as I inched forward, the ledge widened. A miracle! Saved!

I turned and assured my fellow campers that ledges like this usually widened at the far end. "Oh, look! This is where the widening starts. I bet you guys were getting pretty wor-ried! Ha!"

That was the last time I got to lead, which was too bad, because after the ledge I never went anywhere without first assessing the risk. It takes an expert at evaluating risk to even recognize risk in the first place. Take birch trees, for example. Just looking at a slender, graceful birch tree, the average person would never realize it was loaded with risk.

When Vern and I were about twelve, we discovered that a birch tree could give you a decent ride. In those days, we rode everything that was available: horses, cows, pigs, bicycles, wagons, sleds, rafts, and homemade boats. Each contained its own particular kind of treachery, but none measured up to birch trees.

Vern and I would select a birch we thought would give us a decent ride. Then we would climb it until the birch began to bend. Then we would inch up farther and it would bend more. Once we had achieved the right amount of bend, we would let go with our legs and swing out away from the trunk, holding on with our hands. Somewhere I have a poem by Robert Frost titled "A Swinger of Birches." That is what Vern and I were—swingers of birches. Once we had swung out, the tree would begin a graceful bend, lowering us toward the ground. Once we had assessed the risk involved, we would let go simultaneously and drop. Well, actually, we had no other choice at that point.

We swung from so many birches that one day Vern heard his dad say to his mother, "I think our birch trees have some kind of disease. They're all bent over."

Vern didn't say anything. He was an expert at assessing risk.

One day, a new kid moved into our neighborhood and, to make him feel welcome, Vern and I invited him out to swing on birches. I'll call the kid "Hap." I don't remember his real name because he didn't stay long in our neighborhood.

As it turned out, Hap had never swung on birches, and we had to teach him the basics, except for one, which we assumed every kid knows.

Now that there were three of us to swing on birches, we selected a stouter and taller tree than usual. We let Hap go up first, because he claimed to be an excellent tree climber and could teach us some tricks. I was happy to let him lead. Even though I had swung on dozens of birches, this one made me a little uneasy because it was so tall. At last we could feel it begin to bend with the three of us. It bent and bent and bent until we were dangling side by side from beneath the bent portion. We were perhaps eight feet off the ground at that point. Vern, who had assumed command of the operation, said, "OK I'm gonna count out loud, and on the count of three we all let go and drop to the ground. Everybody got it?" Hap and I both answered yes. Vern started counting. "One—two—" at which point he and I let go and dropped to the ground. The birch then snapped up straight and whipped over in the opposite direction!

That's when Hap left the neighborhood. We never saw him again. I think his folks may have thought Idaho was simply too wild a state in which to raise a boy. Vern and I felt bad about Hap. He simply didn't know how to assess the risk of a situation. Any kid should know that when one of the guys says everybody let go on the count of three, everybody lets go on the count of two. It's just common sense. Why Hap wasn't aware of that, I don't know. Maybe he hadn't thought to run a risk assessment on Vern and me.

I often ran risk assessments on Vern but not often enough or thoroughly enough. Once when we were about eight, we were pretending that two holes from which stumps had been blasted were trenches in one of our endless boyhood wars. We lobbed chunks of dried dirt back and forth at each other, the clods bursting harmlessly on one side or the other of us. Incoming clods were easy to dodge. Once, while searching for a suitable clod in the bottom of my foxhole, I glanced up. Vern loomed over me, an immense clod cocked above his head in both hands. KABLOOEY! I almost choked on the cloud of dust that burst around my head. Once again I had failed to run a proper risk assessment, this time on Vern. On the other hand, who would expect an enemy to charge during trench warfare? It was insane.

Learning early about risk assessment has served me well all my life. During my many years as a freelance writer, a photographer and I were accompanying a mountain-climbing expedition for the purpose of doing a TV feature on the venture. At one point we were traversing a steep slope of hard-packed snow. We had to climb down the slope at a steep angle and then proceed back up. The lead climber was stamping footholds in the snow for the long line of climbers following him. I quickly ran a risk assessment and discovered that at the point where the trail angled back up, my feet had to be in the right sequence to match those of the leader. Otherwise, at the sharp turn back up, I would have to leap in the air, switch feet from back to front, and hope I landed in the right footholds when I came down. My risk assessment allowed me to make this necessary adjustment well before I got to the sharp turn. I naturally assumed my photographer would make his own risk assessment. Alas, he didn't. When he came to the turn, he leaped in the air, twisted around, and tried to land in the leader's tracks. He missed, or so I judged from the diminishing "AAAAaaaiii!!" behind me. When I had the opportunity to look back, I could see him zooming down the mountain on his back, his heels sending twin sprays of snow into the air.

I thought, "Just my luck! Now what am I going to do for film?"

I think I must have assessed my first risk at about age eight. My favorite book back then was *The Adventures of Huckleberry Finn*. Huck had run away from home to escape down the Mississippi River on a raft. I would have loved to escape down the Mississippi on a raft, but all I had available was Sand Creek. The creek flowed through the country side for about three miles, then into Lake Pend Oreille, which emptied into the Pend Oreille River, which connected with the Columbia River, which emptied into the Pacific Ocean. I didn't know all that at the time, but actually only wanted to float far enough on Sand Creek that I could still get home before dark. I wasn't in Huck's class when it came to adventure.

My friend Crazy Eddie Muldoon lived on the farm next to ours. Eddie helped me build the raft out of fence posts, which were abundant on his father's farm. The raft turned out to be everything I had imagined except it was rather small. I noticed this when I ran my risk assessment on it. I also noticed that it lacked brakes and a steering wheel. Part of the risk was that I would be at the mercy of the creek and the raft. Eddie seemed to be running his own risk assessment. When I suggested he give the raft a test run, he replied that he couldn't because he was wearing his good pants. The problem with pants for boys in those days was you couldn't tell the good pair from the bad pair. As it happened, I suddenly remembered I was wearing my good pants also. So both of us having made our risk assessments, we shoved the raft off on its journey to the Pacific without a passenger. I was very glad afterward that I'd had the good sense to run that risk assessment. Before the raft had made it around the first bend, it began to disintegrate, each post going its own way. Perhaps it was a design flaw, I don't know.

If one tends to be addicted to adventure, it is important always to assess the risks. Then, of course, you ignore them. Otherwise, it wouldn't be an adventure.

The Forty-Pound Brown Trout

My wife, Bun, has been complaining of late that I can't seem to keep my mind on any single subject for more than five seconds. Nonsense, I say. Now, where was I?

Oh, yes, a while back a reader of mine sent me a colored photo of himself holding a forked stick containing about ten little trout, all eastern brook, as nearly as I could make out. He wrote that he and his son had caught them in a little Idaho lake, the name of which he forgot to divulge. Perhaps he knows I am an eastern brook fanatic.

Brookies are by far the best tasting of all trout. "Tasting!" someone cries out. "You actually eat the fish you catch!" Well, yes, I do, I confess. The recent rise of catch-and-release has made catch-and-eat somehow seem immoral. Fortunately, it appears as if some fish and game departments view the eastern brook trout as somewhat of a lesser fish, because the limit on brookies, (as we aficionados call them) is often set at almost double that of rainbows. I am certainly not in favor of rushing the demise of brookies, but I do appreciate the efforts of fish and game departments to keep the limit on them up to a reasonable eating level. Rainbows, on the other hand, are perfect for catch-and-release, particularly those removed from the hatchery and "planted" by the fish and game department the day before the season opens.

What's that, Bun? Forked sticks? Oh, yeah, I was just getting to that. This report is not about brookies. Don't know how I drifted off onto them. No, what I intended to write about is forked sticks. After brookies, the second thing in the photo to get me excited was the forked stick on which the brookies were strung. When I glimpsed the forked stick, I knew that here were two fishermen of my own ilk or what had once been my ilk. One does not release fish that have been carried about all day on a forked stick, at least not intentionally. In my youth, I occasionally lost a fish from my forked stick, but only because it had dried out, withered, and fallen off on its own. Maybe that's where the whole idea of catch-and-release came from. "Yeah, I had a lot bigger one, but I released it."

There is something to be said for eating the fish you catch. I suspect it has something do with a gene we still retain from the days we actually hunted and fished for food. Undoubtedly, the joy of a kill or a catch was greatly enhanced for anyone who hadn't eaten for a week or two. We still get that little burst of joy from hooking a fish, and I think it may be because we still retain the gene that remembers not having eaten in a couple of weeks.

Fishing is one of those things you don't want to think too much about. I know people with $50,000 boats and about that much in fishing tackle, and they still get that little burst of joy from hooking a fish. Not only could they go to the fish market and buy a whole salmon, but they could buy the whole market. So where does the thrill come from in catching a fish? I don't want to think too much about it.

Now, where was I? Oh, yeah, forked sticks. I guess the reason I was so impressed by the picture of a forked stick strung with brookies was because I hadn't even seen a forked stick in maybe forty years, let alone one strung with little trout.

As a kid, when I first heard about a wicker creel, I thought it was some kind of folk dance. I still have my first wicker creel. It's hanging out in what I laughingly call my shop. As soon as a fisherman obtained his first wicker creel, forked sticks started to fade into history. The fine art of cutting a forked stick from a willow became a lost art. You simply dropped your fish through the little hole in the lid of the creel and that was it. If the fish was too big to fit through the hole, you unfastened the leather strap that held the lid down, opened the basket, and placed the fish inside. There was some technique involved with the creel. Before inserting the first trout, you filled the creel half-full of ferns that you had gotten wet by dunking them in the creek. These helped keep your fish fresh, but also the water leaked out of the creel and ran down your leg keeping it fresh, too. I can still remember the sensation of that water soaking my leg. It wasn't pleasant, but it reminded me that a person had to be tough to put up with all the kinds of hardship you experience as a true fisherman.

The creel that hangs in my workshop was probably the same one that accompanied me on my first hike into the North Fork of Callihan Creek. There was no road into Callihan back then, and the only way to reach the upper creek was for us to hike in over the mountains and then drop down a steep sidehill into the drainage. Callihan was so full of native rainbows that if your fly dropped in the water accidentally while you were wading the creek, you would catch a fish and . . . "What's that Bun? Forked sticks? Oh, yeah, forked sticks."

Forked sticks were a big part of my youth. You never used your forked stick more than once. After you had unthreaded your fish from the stick and dropped the fish in the sink, you tossed the forked stick in the garbage.

Finding a new forked stick, just the right forked stick, was part of the art of fishing in those days. A couple of my friends had a clever way of cutting a forked stick so that it had two forks, one at each end. The upper fork was slipped under the angler's belt and twisted, and that way he didn't have to hold the stick while he fished.

I always carried my forked stick in my hand. This led to major excitement. In order to fish a hole properly, I would lay the forked stick and my catch down on a rock. After I had fished several holes downstream, I would catch another fish and start to thread it on my forked stick. But the stick would be gone! Then I would race back upstream looking for it and at last would find it resting on a rock, the fish drying out and starting to crinkle up. I would dunk them in the creek to freshen them up and then proceed back down the creek. The joy of finding my catch once again greatly improved the quality of my fishing in those days. A fisherman who has never used a forked stick for holding his catch will never know the joy of finding it on a rock two or three times during a day of fishing.

Eventually, I outgrew forked sticks as a means of carrying my catch, but I have never forgotten the art. For one thing, you tried always to remember to carry your jackknife with you whenever you went fishing. That was so you could clean your fish before heading home, a small gesture always appreciated by mothers. Even more important, however, the jackknife simplified and improved the art of preparing the forked stick. True, it was possible to prepare a forked stick by twisting off the willow branch and the fork, but this left the ends fuzzy and hard to slip through the gills and mouth of small trout. A jackknife allowed you to cut the ends at a smooth angle, thereby simplifying the threading on of fish.

Eventually I would grow up and fish in many distant parts of the world, but no such expeditions satisfied me as much as the days spent casting lead sinkers and hooks baited with freshly dug worms into the swirling creeks within walking distance of my boyhood home. It was a rather primitive pastime but highly satisfying.

Then one day in my early thirties a financial windfall suddenly descended on me, my wife, and four young daughters that would have allowed us to buy a house of our own. Instead of giving in to such foolishness, we went off to live in England for several months. It was our first trip abroad, and we did all the usual things: exploring historical sites, museums, castles, restaurants, and I can't remember what all. We were in the land of Izaak Walton, author of *The Compleat Angler*. Although Walton wasn't that great at spelling, he was one of the great authors of his time or any other time, but even more important, he was a man who truly understood fishing. I decided that before I left England I would have to fish in some of the streams that Walton had fished. I'm not sure which streams those were, but in my research I discovered that England possessed a number of fishing hotels. I had never heard of a fishing hotel, but I soon found one within an hour's drive of our temporary place of lodging. The very next day, I arrived at the hotel shortly after the crack of dawn and found the fishing headquarters. The manager quickly rented me a trout "beat," which consisted of a mile or so section on what he referred to as a "river." I cannot recall if I asked him whether Izaak Walton had fished the river, but I'm certain he would have assured me that, indeed, the stream was among Izaak's favorites. In addition to the beat, I also had to rent a complete fishing outfit. The total cost of the fishing gear and the beat came to forty pounds or about $200 at the exchange rate of approximately $5 per pound at the time. Well worth the cost, I must say, to fish the same stream as Izaak Walton had fished.

The fishing manager gave me a little map on which he had circled the section that consisted of my beat. My car now lightened by the cash I had left with the manager, I easily sped to my assigned beat. The stream, which we in the U.S. would refer to as a creek or a crick instead of a river, was nevertheless not without its attractions. There was thick foliage on either side that seemed to extend over the top of the cree—er, river, providing the sensation that the stream flowed through a green tunnel. It would have been impossible to fish from either shore, but the water was no more than a foot deep, and the fishing manager had thoughtfully provided me with a pair of waders.

I thoroughly enjoyed strolling down the middle of the stream and sending my line and fly a dozen yards ahead. Never once disturbed by the irritation of a trout attacking my fly, I found the excursion quite peaceful and easily could imagine Izaak Walton fishing alongside me, only with more luck.

And then suddenly it happened. A tiny fish struck my fly. Somehow I had managed to catch an eight-inch trout before reaching the end of my beat. It was a brown trout. It had cost me exactly forty pounds. Still, I thought it was very strange that a fishing hotel would rent out beats totally lacking in fish with the exception of my one catch. I was not upset. I had experienced fishing in England, perhaps in the very same waters Izaak himself had fished. It was enough. Now, with evening closing in around me, I happened to glance through an opening in the foliage off to my left. Two boys of about twelve were trudging off across a farm pasture. One of them carried a large can, which, I'm sure, contained a supply of worms. The two poachers had gone down creek ahead of me like a seine net, catching every fish but one on my beat! Each of them carried a long string of fish—on forked sticks!

I drove off to our modest cottage, not at all dissatisfied with my day of fishing in England, perhaps in the very same waters as Izaak Walton. Izaak himself, I'm sure, would have been pleased with a forty-pound brown trout. The two boys I had spotted retreating from my "beat" were obviously catch-and-eaters, too, and carried the proof on forked sticks. I couldn't have been more pleased.

Bear Hunters

My friends Retch Sweeney and Birdy Thompson rode home with me on the school bus one crisp Friday afternoon in September. We were going to hunt together over the weekend, and they carried their hunting clothes in large, brown-paper grocery bags. They wore their hunting boots, which by sheer coincidence were also their school boots and their Sunday church boots. In those days, a kid didn't have to waste a lot of time deciding which pair of shoes to wear for which occasion.

Earlier in the week, my mother had driven me around to the Sweeneys and Thompsons to pick up my friends' .30/30 rifles and hunting knives. That was because Ed, the bus driver, didn't want the kids who rode the bus to carry guns and knives. He said it put him at a disadvantage.

In those days, the girls rode on one side of the bus and the boys on the other. Parents and school officials were afraid to have the boys and girls sit together. There's no sense taking chances, they said. The bus was full of the smells and sounds of kids eating snacks they had saved from their school lunches—oranges, slabs of dried pie, hard-boiled eggs, and stale baloney sandwiches. The bus driver used to mutter that the sound of after-school snacks being eaten was sending him to an early grave. Ed did a lot of joking like that.

Every so often, the bus would stop to disgorge kids. Occasionally some kids would be disgorged who didn't want to be disgorged. Whenever a fight erupted, Ed would pull the bus to the edge of the road and order the combatants out. Sometimes they would refuse to leave, and Ed would get up wearily from his driver's seat, walk back, grab them, drag them down the aisle of the bus, and disgorge them forcibly. Then they would have to walk home, usually shaking their fists at the back of the bus. Riding the bus was always interesting as a result of these activities, and Retch and Birdy, both town kids, seemed to enjoy the ride immensely.

"Are you sure your friend Rancid Crabtree doesn't mind us spending the weekend with him?" Birdy asked.

"Sure, I'm sure," I said. "Matter of fact, it was Rancid's idea. He said that way we could get an earlier start on the bear hunt."

Rancid was an old woodsman who lived back against the mountain behind our place. He had taught me everything I knew about hunting and fishing and trapping and a whole lot of other stuff, some of which my mother didn't want me to know, like why the boys and girls didn't get to sit together on the bus.

"Is Rancid going to hunt with us?" Retch asked.

"Nope," I said. "He is just going to drive us up to Ginger Ann's ranch. Ginger Ann's sort of his girlfriend, and he's gonna spend the day there."

"How come he'd rather spend the day there than hunt with us?" Birdy asked.

I just shook my head. I figured Birdy probably didn't know yet why the boys and girls didn't get to sit together on the bus, and it wasn't my place to tell him. "Rancid says there's a good chance we can get us a bear though," I went on. "A bear tore up all of Ginger Ann's beehives this summer. It even killed her pig."

"Killed her pig?" Birdy said.

At that moment, two sixth graders near us got into a fistfight over the ownership of an Oreo cookie, and Ed came back to drag them out of the bus.

"How big a bear did Rancid say it is?" Retch asked, fending off a stray left hook from one of the sixth graders.

Ed got hold of a flailing leg and began to pull, propping his foot against the back of an empty seat.

"He said it was a big one," I said, pushing one of the grunting fighters off my lap. "He said the tracks were big around as dinner plates."

"That's a big bear, all right," Ed put in. "Pat, would you see if you can pry Rupert's fingers loose from that seat leg?"

"You bet," I said, grabbing Rupert by an ear so he couldn't bite me while I worked on his fingers. "You don't suppose it might be a grizzly, do you, Ed, with tracks that big?"

"I hope it's a grizzly!" Rupert yelled.

"Naw, I don't reckon it'd be a grizzly," Ed said. "The last grizzly I seen in these parts was up on the headwaters of Pack River and that was near twenty years ago. Here, let me hold his ear while you get his other hand loose. You know Oscar Davis, how fat he is? I swear Oscar went up a tree so fast it was thirty seconds before most of his fat caught up with him. Most interesting thing I ever seen. Thanks, Pat, I can get him by myself now. C'mon, Rupert, you're walking home."

"Don't mention it," I said.

"We gonna eat at your house tonight?" Retch asked, the sounds of chomping, munching, and slurping apparently having aroused his appetite.

"No, Rancid said he'd fix supper for us."

"What do you suppose he'll cook?" Retch said.

"I can't tell you," I said. "It's supposed to be a surprise."

"Good," Birdy said. "I like surprises."

I didn't say anything. A kid who didn't know why girls and boys couldn't sit together on the bus couldn't know much about surprises either.

When we got to my stop, Retch and Birdy thanked Ed for the ride and all the entertainment. Ed said, "Don't mention it. Sorry it was so dull. Usually we have a little excitement."

We stopped by my house to change our clothes and pick up our rifles and hunting gear and then headed over to Rancid's cabin. The old woodsman was happy to see us. I introduced him to Birdy, Rancid having already met Retch.

"Uh, nice place you got here, Mr. Crabtree," Birdy said, glancing around the cabin.

"Thanks. Ah like it. Pull up an apple box and hev a seat. Jist toss them hides on the floor thar, Retch. Thar's a choppin' block underneath that will make a good seat fer ya. Wall, all be dang! Ah been lookin' all over fer thet ax an' all the time it's bin under thet pile of hides. Place is kind of a mess right now. You wouldn't believe ah cleaned it up jist last March, would ya?"

Rancid poured us each a big steaming cup of coffee, first politely blowing the dust out of Birdy's cup. I could see that Rancid was using his best manners; he usually wiped the dust out of a cup with his shirttail, if he wiped it out at all. Birdy was sort of a finicky guy, though, and didn't seem to fully appreciate Rancid's notion of hygiene. He sneaked me a look that was half question and half accusation.

Rancid set the table with a variety of tin plates, pint jars for glasses, and various other vessels that defied identification. Then he got ready to serve up his surprise. I had experienced enough of Rancid's surprises that my anticipation was mixed with a good measure of anxiety. After all, I didn't want him to serve my friends something they didn't like. Much to my relief, the surprise turned out to be the tiny little cutlets that Rancid favored so much. They were delicious too, and Retch and Birdy just couldn't seem to get enough of them. The fried wild mushrooms were good too, and added just the right amount of excitement to the meal—for me, at least, since I knew Rancid wasn't all that knowledgeable about his wild mushrooms.

"You're positive these mushrooms ain't poisonous?" I asked.

"Why shore ah'm positive. B'sides, ah always fries up a batch beforehand and feeds 'em to maw dog, jist to test 'em out. Hyar, Sport! Come show these fellers you ain't dead! Sport! Gol-dang, whar is thet dog? He always comes when I call. Wall, no matter. Hyar, let me give you another heppin' of mushrooms."

"Here, Sport!" Retch called.

"Sport! Sport!" Birdy yelled.

"Ain't no use calling Sport," I said, giving my friends a serious look. "He ain't going to come."

Rancid shook his head sadly, "No, ah'm afraid he ain't."

"How come he ain't?" Birdy asked in a quavering voice.

"Because there ain't no Sport," I said. "Rancid doesn't have a dog."

We had a good laugh over Rancid's joke and after that we all loosened up, and Rancid had a dose from his jug of rheumatism medicine.

"How is that medicine for rheumatism, Rancid?" Birdy asked, dropping all pretense of formality. "My grandmother's got it pretty bad."

"Wall, ah don't know how it would work fer your granny," Rancid said. "But it shore works fer me. Ah don't have a bit of rheumatism."

We talked way late into the evening, about everything from Rancid's miraculous medicine to why girls and boys don't get to sit together on the bus, the best way to sight in a rifle, and ghosts, several of which Rancid claimed to have seen. He said one of the ghosts had raised such huge goose bumps on him that they left his skin loose all over when they finally died down.

"Speakin' of ghosts," Rancid said. "You know thet b'ar what went an' kilt Ginger Ann's pig?"

"Killed her pig?" Birdy asked.

[65]

"Yeah," Rancid went on. "Wall, ah shore hope thet warn't a ghost b'ar. Ah seed a ghost b'ar only once, but even thet was a time too many. A trapper named Fitz was runnin' a line back up in the Cabinet Mountains. One fall, he hauled some provisions in to his cabin an' didn't come back. Ah went up into the mountains to look fer him. Whan ah come down off the trail in to the Boulder Crick Basin, it started to snow real heavy. All of a sudden, this great big shape rises up ahead of me, must a been ten foot tall. Than the snow let up fer jist a instant and ah seed it was a monster b'ar. Had fangs on it long as railroad spikes and claws the size of ice tongs. Ah could see right through the critter! Wall, sar, ah figgered the only thang to do was to pump about three thutty-ought-six slugs right through it jist to make shore it was really a ghost b'ar, but by the time I got a cartridge in the chamber maw feet had already carried me out of shootin' range. Both maw feet is yeller-bellied cowards when it comes to ghost b'ars."

"Geez!" Birdy said.

"Holy cow!" Retch gasped.

"Never did find ol' Fitz," Rancid went on. "Ah figger the ghost b'ar must of got him. Shore hope thet b'ar what killed Ginger Ann's pig ain't a ghost b'ar."

"Killed her pig?" Birdy said.

"Rancid, I thought you said the bear's tracks were big around as dinner plates," I said. "A ghost bear wouldn't make tracks."

"Mebby so, mebby not," Rancid said. "But if it did, they would be big around as dinner plates."

Shortly thereafter we turned in for the night. Retch and Birdy and I made our bed on the floor, stripped down to our underwear, and climbed under the pile of hides. Rancid got into his bunk and blew out the kerosene lamp as Retch and Birdy studied him with fascination.

"Uh, Rancid," Birdy said after a bit. "Aren't you, uh, gonna take off your boots and clothes?"

"What fer?" Rancid said. "Jist have to put them back on ag'in in the mornin'."

"Yeah, I guess that's right," Birdy said. "I never thought of it that way before."

"That was sure a good supper you fixed us, Rancid," Retch said as we lay there staring up into the dark.

"It sure was," I said, pleased with the fine meal Rancid had cooked in honor of my friends' visit. I was glad that neither Retch nor Birdy had thought to ask what the surprise was.

Early the next morning, Rancid hauled us up to Ginger Ann's ranch, and Retch and Birdy and I hiked up the mountain in search of the bear, leaving Rancid to visit with Ginger Ann. Ginger Ann ran the ranch by herself and frequently suggested to Rancid that she wouldn't mind having a big, strong, energetic man around to help with all the work. Rancid would tell her that if he ever came across such a man, she would be the first to know. I've always thought that Rancid and Ginger Ann probably had one of the world's first meaningful relationships.

The three of us bear hunters climbed steadily for an hour, crossed the ridge of the mountain, and then dropped over into a shallow basin on the far side, where Rancid had told us he thought the bear would be hanging out. We found a set of bear tracks, but they were only about the size of pie plates. Still, they seemed plenty large enough, about the size that makes you turn around every so often to make sure nothing is sneaking up on you from behind.

"Maybe we should spread out a bit," I suggested in a whisper as we worked our way through high brush.

"Good idea," Retch whispered back. "There, how's that?"

"Fine," I said. "Now you're not bumping my arm. Could you spread out a bit too, Birdy?"

"*Woof?*"

"Did you say 'woof'?"

"No, I thought you did."

"I didn't say 'woof.'"

At that moment what had said "woof" reared up on its hind legs a short distance ahead of us and turned in a slow circle, testing the air with its snout.

"A WARSH TUB?" Rancid Crabtree said, spilling his coffee on Ginger Ann's table. "Its haid was as big as a warsh tub?"

"*Choke! Gasp! Wheeze!*" I said. "Yes . . . *gasp* . . . big . . . *gasp* . . . as a wash tub!"

"Eyes . . . *wheeze* . . . like red fire!" Retch added.

"Could see . . . *choke* . . . right . . . *gasp* . . . through it!" Birdy put in.

"How long ago was you seed it?" Rancid asked, thoughtfully scratching the stubble on his jaw.

"About . . . *gasp* . . . five minutes ago . . . *gasp* . . . in that basin . . . *choke* . . . on the other side of the mountain!"

Ginger Ann smiled at Rancid. "Sounds like that ghost bear you're always talking about. You'd better get a rifle, and go see if it really is a ghost bear."

Rancid glared at her in his comical bug-eyed manner. "Wall, dang if ah would, woman, if ah had the time. But ah jist thought of some important business ah near forgot about. Mebby next week . . ."

Later that fall, Ginger Ann herself killed a bear on the mountain. She said its head wasn't as big as a wash tub but more the size of a milk pail. Its eyes weren't like red fire, either, and as far as she could tell, the bear was impossible to see through. That was how we knew it wasn't the same bear that had reared up practically on top of us. For all I know, the ghost bear is still prowling around up on Ginger Ann's mountain, even though nobody has reported seeing it since.

Riding the bus back to school on Monday morning, Retch and Birdy both agreed that they had had a fine time and had learned a whole lot from the weekend spent in the country with Rancid Crabtree.

"Say, what was them delicious little cutlets Rancid fed us for supper?" Retch asked as we bounced along in the back of the bus.

"Yeah, they were good," Birdy said. "What were they?"

I told them about the surprise, and they reacted exactly the way I had expected.

Fortunately, we were only a couple of miles from school at the time. Even then I myself probably could have ridden the rest of the way on the bus, if that dirty little Rupert hadn't helped Ed pry my fingers off the seat leg.

A Lake Too Far

Some hunters and anglers tend to think of birders as wimps, persons afraid of adventure. Far from it! I hunt and fish, but I also bird, and I'm a macho kind of guy, if ever there was one. Birding can lead to some tough adventures. Here's an example.

Once while searching for exotic birds to watch, my friend Retch Sweeney and I were walking down a beach on an island off the coast of Australia. Suddenly, we came upon a lady relaxing on a chaise longue and calmly reading a book. She wore not a stitch! This was not the sort of situation we were accustomed to finding ourselves in on a beach, although an occurrence apparently not that rare on islands off a coast of Australia. Retch and I gave a startled jump and took off running, I guess because both of us thought we had wandered into some place we were not supposed to be. I do remember the lady lowering her book and glowering at us. As I recall, Retch had gasped out some colorful expression. To show how shocked I was, I didn't even notice the title of the book the lady was reading. It was a small paperback, though, I'm pretty sure about that. So how many hunters and anglers run into a naked lady on a beach? Not that many, I bet.

Whoa! I started writing about how tough birding is and drifted off into recollection. Not only am I a very macho birder, I'm easily distracted. Here I was thinking about birds one second and a naked lady on a beach the next. My mind had even gone blank for a second, but I remember now. The naked lady occurred on the same trip in which Bun and I had heard about a lake in the far Outback of Australia. It was reported to contain a huge population of exotic birds. We figured that in one fell swoop we could triple our life lists with all the birds of Australia.

I asked the manager at a car rental place in Sydney how to get to the lake. "We're birders," I told him.

"Sorry to hear that, mate," he said. "How come you want to go to Far Outback Lake?"

I can't remember the lake's actual name, but it was something like that, only in Australian.

"We like adventure," Bun told him.

The man nodded. "You'll get your fill of it out there."

"Can you tell us how to find it?"

"You can't miss it. There's only one road goes in that direction."

"I see," I said. "How do I find that road?"

"Take your first turn to the right after you cross the Blue Mountains."

"And how far then to the lake?"

"About five hundred miles, but the people who live out that way drive it pretty fast. You, on the other hand, might not want to go much over eighty. One thing I should mention, though. The traffic on the road is two-lane."

"That doesn't bother me," I said.

"The road is one-lane."

"That bothers me," I said.

"Yep, that does bother some folks new to the area. The way it works, say you got two cars approaching each other from opposite directions. The driver headed north drops his two left tires in the ditch on his side and the driver headed south drops his two left tires into the ditch on his side, and the two cars pass each other just fine. The highway department has smoothed out the ditches on each side to accommodate passing."

"I see."

"Don't worry yourself about passing, son. You'll get use to it in no time."

"Right."

Australia's Blue Mountains are as pretty as any you'll see in the United States, and we took most of a day driving over them. I was occasionally distracted by the screeching as we rounded some of the sharp curves. I personally don't recall screeching myself, but Bun handled that task well enough on her own. The next time we go adventuring in Australia, we will definitely go by train. So I am happy we had the opportunity to see some of that continent's mountains in all their pristine beauty while we were still young.

Oh, I should mention here that we completed our journey over the Blues with the car in the same perfect condition in which we had rented it.

Shortly after we arrived at the turnoff, we came to a combination of connected buildings consisting of a gas station, café, and motel, all neatly fitted together. As I recall, the price of regular gas was about thirty-five cents per gallon, to give you an idea of how far in the past this was. An attractive lady came out and pumped the gas, checked the oil, and washed the windshield—that gives you another idea of how far back in the past it was.

We then went into the café to eat. A lady identical to the one at the gas station came out to take our order, except this lady wore an apron. After she left, I started to hum the theme song from *The Twilight Zone*, but Bun shushed me. I assumed the gas station lady had a twin. It was also my impression that the waitress also did all the cooking.

After dinner, we walked next door to the motel. A third identical lady came out of the back of the building to rent us a room. As far as I could determine, a set of triplets ran the whole complex. It was really quite astonishing that three women could handle this entire operation by themselves, but Australians are a tough and vigorous people, and I don't recall a single time we came across a person who might be regarded as a sluggard.

As I was checking out the next morning, one of the motel triplets asked what had brought us out that way.

"We're birders," I told her.

"I'm sorry," she said.

At one small ranch town, we went into a general store to buy an authentic Australian cowboy hat so I would resemble the other hardened individuals we met along the way. The clerk who waited on us recognized me as an American right off—I don't know how—and started asking all kinds of questions about life in the United States. I was happy to oblige. Soon, a small crowd had gathered around to listen to my lecture, and I could tell they were impressed, despite a certain rude scoffing from my spouse. After they heard we were on our way to Far Outback Lake to look at birds, though, they seemed to lose interest. Apparently, bird watching is not a big outdoor activity in the Australian Outback.

As the rental car manager had explained, the road to Far Outback Lake consisted of a fairly smooth layer of dirt that sloped gradually into the ditch on each side. The standard procedure for passing consisted of each driver putting the two tires on the left side of his car down in the ditch shortly before passing. The driver in the approaching car often slowed down to eighty miles an hour or so. (You have to travel very fast if you want to get anywhere in Australia.) I never quite got the hang of passing head-on traffic at eighty miles an hour, so as soon as I spotted another vehicle approaching, I headed for the ditch, and we sat there until the other driver shot by in the opposite ditch. You might think that one would become accustomed to this method of passing head-on traffic, and one does, of course, but not until one is a nervous wreck.

Here I should mention something about Outback vehicles. Each of them seems to come equipped with thick iron bars in front of the radiator. Rental cars from Sydney, such as ours, do not come equipped with such bars. Early on, I asked one of the Outback residents about this accessory.

"Oh, you mean roo-bars."

"Roo-bars?" I said.

"Yes, indeed. Out here, you quite often hit kangaroos while driving. The roo-bars keep the beasts from wiping out your vehicle."

"Oh," I said. "Well, I certainly have no intention of hitting a kangaroo."

"Good luck with that, mate."

After traveling five hundred or so miles across Australia, we at last arrived at what appeared to be a sandy desert. It looked like the sort of place where we might find a lake, and I sent Bun into a gas-station-café-and-motel combination to ask for directions. I would have gone in myself, but I was afraid I might run into one of the triplets.

When Bun returned, she reported that she had asked the lady at the counter where we might find the lake. The lady pointed to the sand outside the window and said, "That's it."

"Oh, dear," Bun said to her. "We drove all this way to see the birds."

The lady shook her head. "No birds here, I'm afraid. You should have come after a wet."

"When was the last wet?" Bun asked.

"Seven years ago."

We eventually met up with Retch and his wife. They don't care much for birding but had been exploring expensive restaurants and numerous resorts near Sydney. They had no trouble persuading Bun to give up birding in exchange for their kind of adventure. Some people simply aren't cut out for the hazards of serious birding.

Oh, I should also report on the condition of the rental car when I turned it in. Both headlights and the windshield were broken. All the wheel covers had been knocked off, and there were multiple dents randomly distributed about the car. Most of the trim was still intact, if somewhat rearranged. Bun's faculties were also pretty much intact, if somewhat rearranged. Most of the damage was concealed under numerous layers of dirt. Fortunately, I'd had the foresight to add several extra layers of insurance on the car, so the car rental company would be made whole.

Bun said, "You better clean off all that kangaroo blood."

I refused. How many Americans ever get to turn in a rental car, one side of which is smeared with kangaroo blood? I am happy to report, though, that the kangaroo was already dead before we hit it. Still, it was a scary situation. The next time I drive in the Australian Outback, I'm definitely going to be equipped with roo-bars. Maybe I'll even get a set for the car.

The Chicken Chronicles

Most people nowadays never have a close relationship with chickens and so never get to know them as individuals. My very first memory involves chickens. I was probably about two years old and was wandering around the backyard of our old farmhouse. I was stark naked. For some unknown reason, I had taken off all my clothes, possibly because it was summer and very hot. The family's free-roam chickens gathered around, clucking and squawking and seemingly accepting me as one of their own. I came across the chickens' water pan and sat down in it. I can recall quite distinctly that the water was warm and very pleasant. The chickens gathered around, expressing great interest in me, clucking excitedly and cocking their heads this way and that. Apparently, they had never seen anyone sit in their water pan before. It was at that moment that my grandmother happened to look out the front window of the house and saw a car coming down our long driveway. Having already observed me in the backyard, she certainly did not want visitors to see a member of the family sitting stark naked in the chickens' watering pan. She flew out of the house, scooped me up under one arm, and rushed back into the house. Later that day she had a stroke, for which I was forever after blamed. Gram and I were very close from that day until her death many years later. So you can see that chickens can create binding relationships.

Our chickens and other livestock were not kept as pets. They were expected to earn their keep, often giving up their lives in that effort. Until I went off to college, there was not a single time I can remember that we did not have chickens at the farm.

I imagine that farm life today isn't all that different from suburban life, except perhaps there is more distance between neighbors. In the farm days of my youth, an immense amount of killing went on, the victims being chickens, rabbits, hogs, steers, even fish, deer, and just about any wild creature that wandered by.

Even when I was still very young, my grandmother would stand by the chopping block and tell me, "Run down that chicken for me." It seemed the chickens were less afraid of me than of Gram. It was easy for me to imagine them yelling, "Run for your lives! Here comes that crazy old lady with the ax."

Many years later, after I had become a professor and we lived in the suburbs, we kept a family of bantam chickens, which our daughters named Verde, Gladys, Mabel, and Ralph, the first two after aunts, the third after their grandmother, and the fourth after an uncle. They said they were perfect chicken names, an opinion we did not pass on to the adults who owned the names.

One spring, I took the family off with me to Mexico, where I had a job teaching at a university, and when we returned the chickens had vanished. None of our neighbors or friends nor our housesitter could explain what had happened to them. I guess there are just some people who don't appreciate chickens. I, on the other hand, have long taken the trouble to distinguish them as individuals.

To most people, I assume, all chickens pretty much look alike, and they are therefore incapable of distinguishing them as individuals. I suppose they think there is no difference between chopping off a chicken's head and eating him or her, and chopping off Ralph's head and eating him. There is a big difference. Once a chicken has distinguished himself as an individual, he or she is pretty safe, at least from my hands. Nobody would feel comfortable eating Ralph.

A local columnist for a newspaper, a friend of mine, has had great success in writing about a chicken who roams her neighborhood. That chicken has become famous in our town. If the column goes too long without a report on "Chicken," readers become concerned. I think their concern has something to do with identity. Once you are distinguished from the herd—or the flock, in this case—people view you differently, even if you are only a chicken. Walt Whitman, the poet and mystic, wrote, "Once you have been identified, you are saved." I think that is true, even for chickens. I doubt any readers of the column will ever forget Chicken. If you are undistinguishable in a crowd of a thousand, no one is particularly concerned about turning you into nuggets.

Many of our chickens ended up as Sunday dinners, while others earnestly laid eggs as quickly as they could, while keeping an eye out for the crazy old lady with the ax. Several, however, did distinguish themselves as individuals and were saved. One that comes to mind is Old Biddy, my mother's name for a little, white hen. While Mom was shucking corn, say, on the back porch, Biddy would wander over and talk to her.

"So, how are you today, Biddy?" Mom would ask.

Biddy would reply, with clucks and squawks, perhaps telling Mom of her latest adventures.

For some reason, Biddy took it upon herself to become the protector of the family, attacking anyone walking down

our driveway that she didn't recognize. One day I was walking out to the highway when I came across two shoes, both
pointed away from the house and a long stride apart. As we
learned later, a girlfriend of my sister's was coming over for
a visit when Biddy attacked her. The girl turned around and
ran right out of her shoes. No doubt Biddy had recognized
the girl was up to no good and presented a significant danger
to the family.

My grandmother was not the only threat to the lives of our
free-roam chickens. Every spring, some of our hens would
come plodding out of the brush followed by a string of little
yellow puffballs that had been hatched out in the wilds. Mom
decided they needed more protection from the elements, which
included skunks and weasels. So she built them half a dozen
little lean-tos in which to spend the night. It probably was my
job to close the entrances on the lean-tos, but apparently one
night I forgot. Mom heard a terrible racket outside and rushed
out to save her chickens. She dropped on her knees in front
of one of the lean-tos, slipped her hand under the hen, and set
it off to one side, trying to see what all the ruckus was about.
Then she realized the hen wasn't a hen but a skunk. The
skunk didn't spray her, but rushed off without firing a single
shot. I've always thought that the skunk was so impressed
by someone who calmly picked him and set him aside that it
decided she was not a person to mess with. And he was right,
of course.

I do not care all that much for county fairs, except
I do like to stop by and watch the baby pigs perform. After
that, I walk over to the chicken pavilion. The chickens seem
uncomfortable to be on display in cramped, little cages.
Somehow they seem to recognize me, perhaps from another
life, when I spent a hot afternoon sitting in their drinking
water. They smile and nod, although it takes a great admirer
to recognize when a chicken is smiling.

Secret Athlete

My athletic prowess may not weigh heavily on the minds of potential world champions, but that is because they have never heard of me or it. Once word gets out though, they won't sleep nights for worry.

I am that rarity in the world of sport—the secret athlete. Even my family and friends don't suspect they live in close proximity to the unofficial world-record-holder in more track-and-field events than they have ever heard of. They think all I do is fish, a sport popularly regarded as mild therapy for outpatients from the geriatric ward.

Most of my acquaintances are under the impression that I would get shin splints from a fast game of Monopoly. I'm said to get short of breath ascending the north face of a bar stool. People joke that my only form of exercise is elbow-bending. (Seriously though, you never know when you might break a leg and have to crawl out of the wilderness on your elbows.)

The reason for these false impressions about my fitness is the clever disguise I've perfected over a number of decades, essentially the appearance of a gray-haired, middle-aged guy shaped like a yam. But as I recently revealed to my wife, Bun, beneath the flab hides the rock-hard body of a world-class athlete.

"*Whose?*" she exclaimed. "I hope it doesn't belong to anybody I know!"

I mention Bun's pitiful attempt at sarcastic wit only as an indication of my fantastic disguise. "Why, it may be asked, do I hide my sleek, rippling physique from the eyes of the world?" Quite simply, it is to avoid the attention of wild, wanton, beautiful women and their come-hither looks, not to mention the endless pestering of male fashion magazines for me to act as a model of their latest fashions. It would all be so very boring and, most important, a distraction from my pursuit of a really big fish.

For me, stepping into a pair of waders is a lot like Clark Kent stepping into a phone booth. *Is it a bird? Is it an airplane? Is it a flying yam? No, it is Super Athlete!*

Just recently, for example, I ran a 100-yard dash in 9.5 seconds. I would have done much better if I had been wearing only a pair of shorts and track shoes, instead of being fully clothed in a pair of hip boots (one of which was half-full of water) and carrying a fly rod, a creel, a landing net, and five pounds of fishing tackle.

The time for the herd of cows was about a minute five, but they had trouble getting organized and properly aligned on my track. I think one of them was a bull, but I'm not sure. Usually, I can identify a bull right away because he is the one who smiles when he sees a fisherman. The only thing that prevented the race from becoming a cross-country event was a fence at the end of the pasture.

Sadly, the fisherman-athlete must learn to live without the slightest recognition, let alone fame. Millions of sports fans thrill at the sight of an Olympic runner crossing the finish line, but a fisherman fighting a five-pound rainbow can be swept over a twenty-foot waterfall, do a one-arm backstroke through a hundred yards of of No. 5 rapids, crawl out on a beach, and land his fish, but if there is a single spectator on hand, he will be another fisherman who will ask, "What kind of fly you using?"

One of my specialties is the sitting broad jump. Fishermen with a preference for high mountain streams perform this event with practiced skill, although even a beginner usually does fairly well at it. I once saw a plump, middle-aged fisherman scoot himself out on a log extending over a nice, deep pool thirty feet or so beneath him. The log suddenly snapped in two. Even an experienced high-mountain fisherman might have ridden it down, but this gentleman somehow flexed his rear in such a manner as to propel himself back to solid ground.

"Nice recovery," I said.

"Thanks," he said.

"You done fishing that hole?" I asked.

"Yeah," he said. "I think I'll go take a nap."

Clearly, he was new to the snapped log event, which often takes a new angler some time to recover. I eased out on what remained of the log and managed to get a couple of casts in before a loud crack sent me into the double back flip while tying on a new fly. The "crack" was nothing more than the popping of an inflated sack by the previous occupant of the log. Although he was doubled over in a fit of mirth, I was not amused. Fishing high-mountains streams is serious business.

The beaver-hole drop can be one of the most exciting of angling events, particularly to observers and any beavers in the area. Usually, the event takes the angler completely by surprise. There are two kinds of beaver-hole drops, the one-legger and the two-legger. The two-legger is rather neat and might be graded on style alone, depending on the vocalization of the droppee. The one-legger is by far the most difficult. One leg is inserted up to the confluence of the body, while the other leg runs around on the surface. The expression of concern on the droppee's face can be amusing to the observer, but there is a serious side to the one-legger, depending on whether the beaver is home at the bottom of the hole.

A couple of years ago, I participated in the fisherman's version of the decathlon, including the dash, low and high hurdles, and a concluding broad jump to the finish line or, two be more precise, the door of my car. It's tough holding the lead over a swarm of yellow jackets, but I managed to come in first in a field of five hundred. There was at least one cheater in the event, a small but cheeky fellow who apparently hitchhiked on my hat. I rewarded his ingenuity with a swat from a rolled-up newspaper. He made the front page, but I didn't even get a mention in the sports section.

The McManus Principles

I'm often accused of being without principle, but that accusation is unfounded. Not only do I have numerous principles, but I have devoted a considerable amount of time to the perfection of each. Consider, for example, my application of one such principle to a particularly exasperating situation.

My friend Rupert and I were fishing Deep Creek, a very slippery stream, when a large trout rose next to the far bank and made a tentative pass at my fly. He had shown a good deal of enthusiasm in the attempt, and I was sure he would make another try in a matter of seconds. At that very moment, Rupert, having detected the trout himself, pushed past me and was just about to cast when he slipped and went down with a crash and a loud yelp, the yelp apparently the result of his tailbone connecting with a rock. Even though the yelp was made underwater and was somewhat difficult to decipher, I assumed it was some complaint about his tailbone. It later turned out that the bone was not broken or injured in any way, but you would not have known so from the expression on Rupert's face as he stared up at me from beneath the water. He showed not the slightest concern that he might have frightened off my fish. Even though I was certain the monster trout had fled downstream, I made a couple of futile casts over the top of Rupert, ignoring his expression of accusation, distorted somewhat by the depth of water. You would think his slip had been my fault!

The McManus Principle, now in play, raised the question of whether I should immediately criticize Rupert for frightening off my fish or wait until he emerged from his watery retreat. In any case, when he at last resurfaced his whole concern was for his tailbone. I have a tailbone myself, but it has never been of much service to me, and even if it were the finest tailbone in the whole world, I would never have carried on like Rupert. He apparently prized his a great deal and went on and on about it, but at such a high pitch I couldn't detect any particular details about its grandeur.

Being a person of principle, I did not utter even a small criticism of his outburst nor of the fact that he had frightened off the largest trout I had ever seen in Deep Creek. Some people are simply insensitive to the misfortunes of others, and it does no good to recite principles to them. In this case, the McManus Principle is: Never immediately criticize a person whose clumsiness possibly caused you to lose a monster trout because you might seem overly cross at that moment. Simply cast over the top of him, just in case another huge trout might be against the far bank. Remember, alway save your criticism of the villain until later, when you will be much less irritated.

Modesty is yet another of my principles. I make a point of concealing my various talents from those persons accompanying me on various sporting ventures. For example, I deliberately miss easy shots, simply to make my companions feel better about their own inept marksmanship. As a result, I am often invited to accompany other sportsmen on adventures all over the world, with the possible exception of lion hunting.

People whose primary exercise consists of making money often have avoided more athletic pursuits, and, therefore cannot be expected to have acquired the skills I myself possess. So I go to great trouble to appear inept while I am in their company. Indeed, if you happen to run into any of my regular companions, they may very well mention how I am constantly borrowing tackle from them on fishing trips, because I have forgotten certain items of mine—a fishing rod for example. Indeed, they may display some glee in reciting my misadventures, completely unaware that those misadventures were deliberate on my part, simply to make my companions feel better about their own ineptness.

Principles have weight. Most people don't know that. I suppose I do, because my many principles tend to collect mostly around my waist. That at least helps to keep the fat off.

I estimate that the average principle weighs about five pounds. If you have four of them, you are carrying around an extra twenty pounds more than the unprincipled person. I have never counted up my principles, but I must have a lot of them, and they tend to slow me down. In fact, as I progress into my later years, I think I must be putting on even more principles all the time.

There's probably no need to point out that if you are an outdoors person, unprincipled hunters and anglers will beat you at hunting and fishing every time, because they don't have to put up with all that extra weight. I think this acquisition of principles is true in other endeavors as well as outdoor pursuits. It sometimes seems to me that folks lacking in principles often outperform the rest of us in the pursuit of better positions at work and perhaps even in love, but I don't know. They often do seem to soar above the rest of us and rise through the ranks at greater speed than ourselves, perhaps because they are so light on their feet.

I must admit that at times I have thought of dropping a few of my principles but concluded that would be to my detriment. Principles, after all, do have a therapeutic effect. They help you sleep better at night.

Basic Lying Made Easy

B ert Tipple, a local scientist, told me the other day that a recent study of his showed that the average outdoorsman actually takes more time and care in selecting his spouse than he does in selecting his hunting companions. I was shocked.

"That's hard to believe," I said. "Most potential wives don't even come armed."

"It's true, though," Tipple said. "A man is just going to be more careful in his selection of the person he is going to share most of his life with."

"That's my point exactly. So how come you figure he selects his wife with more care than he does his fishing and hunting pals?"

When I got home, I told my wife about the results of Tipple's research. She laughed herself sick. "I can't believe it," she said, wiping away tears of mirth. "And Bert calls himself a scientist. Someone must have pulled the plug on his computer."

"Yeah," I said. "You know how much time I spend checking out prospective hunting and fishing companions. A person can't be too careful about a serious matter like that. Make one little mistake, and you can end up with a real dud."

"You're telling me!" Bun said.

One of the qualities I treasure in Bun is that she's so agreeable.

"Come to think of it," I mused. "I guess I've made my share of mistakes in picking hunting and fishing companions. Boy, some of them were real doozies."

"Which reminds me," Bun said, "your old buddy Retch Sweeney called this afternoon."

"Oh, yeah? What did he want?"

"He said he wanted to remind you about the fishing trip, and that when you come to pick him up to bring an extra fly rod and waders, the rubber raft, the grub and beverage, and the bail money."

"Bail money?"

"Yes, apparently he and another gentleman got into an altercation down at Kelly's Bar & Grill, and Retch was sitting on the man, tickling him under the arms to get him to say 'Enough!' when he noticed the badge on the man's vest."

"Badge?"

"Yeah. What's a SWAT team anyway?"

"A SWAT team?"

"Yes. Do you think it's a serious offense to lock a SWAT team in the ladies' john? I couldn't make heads or tails of what he was saying, he was laughing so hard. Anyway, my impression was there wouldn't have been any problem if the prowl car he borrowed hadn't run out of gas just north of the city limits. What do you make of it?"

"Same ole, same ole," I said. "He's lying."

Really fine outdoor companions like Retch Sweeney don't just grow on trees, although some persons would argue the point, Bun being one of them. I, of course, deserve some credit for making Retch what he is today. Believe it or not, he used to be a loud-mouthed, belligerent oaf who spent all his time eating, drinking, bowling, fighting, lying, gambling, hunting, and fishing.

One day I reached the point where I couldn't stand it anymore and told him he had better knock it off.

"Geez," he said in a hurt tones. "What don't you like?"

"The bowling," I said. "Actually, I can tolerate bowling. It's the bowlers, I can't stand."

I'm happy to report that Retch gave up the bad habit instantly and hasn't bowled in fifteen years.

I must confess I haven't been so lucky in the selection of all my hunting and fishing companions. I've had my share of slackers and sluggards, boors and bores, know-it-alls, nitpickers, lunatics, and lummoxes. Each of these characters in his own right was a master of disguise, who revealed his true self to me only after the last vestiges of civilization had disappeared far behind us.

I remember one chap who pretended to be a ball of energy while we were loading the car for a trip into the wilderness. "Here, let me load that canoe for you. No, no, I can handle it myself. I'll just slip it up there on the rack all by myself, no trouble at all."

The only time he bothered to lift a hand after that was when the camp cook asked who wanted seconds.

While most of these characters were your standard dyed-in-the-wool misfits, two individuals in particular continue to occupy a special place in my memory.

As with all of the aforementioned mistakes in my judgment of character, a chap I'll call Ned managed to win my confidence and admiration by passing himself off as an average human being. The flaw he somehow managed to conceal until we were two days into a week-long canoe trip. I was cooking our breakfast the first morning out, when he squinted through the smoke and asked, "Have you heard the one about the two campers?"

I said I hadn't.

So he told me the joke about the two campers. It was a very funny joke, and I laughed and laughed, little realizing that my response would turn loose a monster. I even thought, what a delight it is to camp out with a man who actually knows how to tell a joke.

But scarcely had I finished wiping my eyes with my handkerchief than he said, "I bet you haven't heard the one about the eyes and handkerchief. Well, it seems . . . " and away he went with another joke. It was funny, too. By the fifth joke in the endless series, I had exhausted all my joke mirth, even though I continued to laugh at each one, simply to be polite.

"It's getting late," I said. "We had better get the canoe loaded."

"Wait! Wait!" he cried, grabbing my arm. "You're going to love this one. It seems . . . "

The deluge of jokes continued for the rest of the trip. If we were shooting at rapids, dodging rocks, fighting the grasp of a whirlpool, I would hear over the roar of the water, "Hey, Pat, you'll love this one. It seems . . . "

I think the only safe way to select an outdoor companion is to hook him up to a lie detector.

You: "Do you tell jokes?"

Candidate: "No, I hate jokes."

You: "OK, you pass."

Candidate: "I should mention that I fatally wounded my last two hunting companions."

You: "No problem. You pass."

One other thing I've learned is that when you are hunting with a new companion, never tell him the truth. When I was young and didn't know any better, I worked in a public relations firm. One day I mentioned something about deer season opening soon. "Hey, great, another hunter!" the fellow next to me said. "I've just taken it up! What say we go deer hunting together?"

"Well, all right," I said. He seemed decent enough. Now even though I worked in public relations, I felt one should always tell the truth when asked a question. Yes, yes, I know now that that is really stupid, but I was about to get a lesson in lying. Never, never lie halfway. It will do you no good. If you're going to lie, go full throttle with the biggest one you can come up with.

One day, Fred, as I'll call him, asked me to join him and his girlfriend for lunch. I said sure. We met the girlfriend at the restaurant. I managed to conceal my shock. Agnes was the homeliest girl I had ever seen. She turned out to be very nice, and I ended up liking her a great deal.

A week later, Fred and I headed up into the mountains on our first hunt together. He was driving. Off on my side of the car, the mountain dropped off sharply. I imagined the wheels of the car occasionally knocking rocks off into space. That's when Fred turned to me and asked out of the blue, "Say, what did you think of my Agnes' looks?"

I must admit I was startled by such a personal question. My public relations background should have come to my rescue, in which case I would have said, "Why, she's gorgeous! She should be in films! I can't imagine what she's doing with a homely guy like you." And so on. Instead of lying through my teeth, I lied just a little bit.

"She's not so bad," I said, gazing out the window into the distance and trying to be kind.

Fred almost drove off the mountain.

We swerved this way and that, sometimes out in empty space and then back on the highway again, and so on. Finally, Fred shouted. "Not so bad! Not so bad! Why she's beautiful!'

So what do I know! Beauty must actually be in the eye of the beholder.

That's something to remember when you're going to spend a night out in the mountains with a guy armed with a loaded gun. Tell full-blown lies and never back off even for a second, even when your hunting companion asks what you think of his girlfriend's looks. Even if she is the most beautiful girl you have ever seen, improve on her startling beauty and do so generously. You will still fall short, but never so far as saying, "Not so bad."

The same goes for the camp cook. When he says, "How was breakfast?" you say it was the best breakfast you have eaten in your entire life.

He says, "I thought the fried potatoes were a little overdone."

You say, "Not at all. I loved the crunching sound they make."

Unless you actually enjoy camp cookery and want to take it up yourself, tell the camp cook his meals are the best thing you've eaten since you last visited France. Indeed, come to think of it, his cooking puts those French chefs to shame, particularly his bacon flambé. So you've never been to France—what's the problem?

Hardly anyone knows how to tell a decent lie anymore, and if it weren't for politicians and fishermen the sport might die out altogether. What really frightens me, though, is that recently I have run across a number of younger anglers who don't seem to have the slightest notion about even the fundamentals of good lying, let alone know anything about the relationship of lying to fishing.

One young fellow, for example, was telling me about how he had this nice trout almost netted, when it suddenly threw the hook and got away. Since he was so young, I decided to play straight man for him.

"How big was he, Bob?" I asked.

"Oh, I'd say nearly two pounds."

"Two pounds?" I said.

He backed off a little. "Well, maybe only a pound and a half."

"A pound and a half!" I yelled. "Nobody has a fish get away that weighs only a pound and a half!"

"They don't?"

"Of course they don't," I said. "I myself never allow a fish to get away that weighs less than five pounds. Usually they weigh a whole lot more. If they weigh less, you might as well keep them."

Bob didn't even know what I was talking about. "No lie?" he said.

"No lie?" I cried. "Of course, a lie! What do you think fishing is all about anyway?"

"Catching fish?"

I shook my head solemnly. "The greatest joy in fishing comes not from the fish you catch, but from the lies you tell about the ones that got away."

He seemed deeply moved by those simple words and said he had never heard that before. Then I could see that I had been a little hard on him. It wasn't that he didn't care about learning proper lying but that he just hadn't been raised right and lying had been left out of his education.

"Didn't your old man teach you any lying when he was showing you how to fish?" I asked kindly.

Bob became indignant. "My father doesn't lie!"

"Not your father," I said. "Fathers don't teach their kids to lie. I mean your old man."

"What old man?"

"Every kid has an old man," I said. "If he's really lucky, he'll have a dirty old man. How else would he learn to spit between his teeth, roll his own smokes, cuss properly, and lie?"

"I missed out, I guess," Bob said. "Nope, I didn't have an old man, dirty or otherwise . . . "

There was the problem. You just have to feel sorry for a youngster who has been deprived like that. It occurred to me that maybe the population is getting so out of whack that there aren't enough old men to go around anymore. I decided to do what I could for Bob and sat him down right there on a rock and proceeded to give him a short course in the fine art of lying.

"I don't like the idea of lying," Bob said.

I nodded. "I can understand that. Lots of folks like yourself simply don't have the proper upbringing. I tell you what, Bob, I'll teach you how to speak the truth that works just like a lie—even better, sometimes."

"I don't understand."

"It works like this. Let's say you come back from a fishing trip and somebody asks, 'How did you do?'"

"'Terrible,' you say, telling the truth. 'I didn't catch a fish over twenty pounds.'"

"Twenty pounds," Bob said. "I've never caught a fish over twenty pounds."

"Right. So you're telling the truth. But the fellow you're talking to will think you normally catch fish over twenty pounds, and that's why you appear disappointed. But you haven't told even an itty-bitty lie, have you?"

"I guess not."

"Well, there you go, Bob."

"I wish I'd had an old man."

I smiled. "Tell you what. I'm not quite an old man yet, but I've been thinking about getting into the business. Maybe I'll practice on you, Bob."

"Gee, that's great, if you can teach me to lie without really lying."

I patted him on the shoulder. "Creative lying is just the start of what you can learn from an old man," I said. "I have a lot of work to do on you, Bob, I can see that. We'd better get started. I'll probably even be an old man by the time I'm done."

A Chainsaw Kind of Guy

Barney Wapshot's wife gave him a chainsaw for Christmas. I was furious. Barney is not a chainsaw kind of guy. It's unlikely he will ever use it to make chainsaw comments to guys at his golf club: "I was going to crank up my chainsaw the other day and cut down a few trees, but then some guests showed up for drinks and hors d'oeuvres by the pool." I hate that sort of pretense, particularly in a guy whose wife gave him the chainsaw in the first place. If you're a real chainsaw kind of guy, you go out and buy your own.

Whatever on earth prompted Winnie, that's his wife, to give Barney a chainsaw, I don't know. Maybe she was sending him a message like, "I wish you were more like Pat—he's a chainsaw kind of guy."

Or maybe Winnie was thinking about the economy. Anytime the economy goes to heck in a handbasket, people start thinking about chainsaws, and how they could go out in a national forest and cut enough firewood to last through the winter: "At least we'll be warm, even if we have to huddle around the fireplace."

Winnie would certainly be right if she thought I was a chainsaw kind of guy. In fact, I have two chainsaws. Three, if I count the electric. The electric's OK for trimming limbs around the house, but totally useless for cutting firewood out in a national forest, unless you have an awfully long extension cord. Besides that, it makes only a wimpy little sound rather than a decent roar.

The other two saws are gas models, but one of them is broken. Actually, it may not be broken, because I took it apart and repaired it myself. On the other hand, you don't want a chainsaw to explode on you. Those saw teeth flying all over the place can really hurt, particularly if you're not a chainsaw kind of guy.

What happened was that my chainsaw was spewing gas all over the place, which alerted me to the possibility that something might be wrong. I should point out here that no chainsaw kind of guy ever wants to take his saw into a chainsaw repair shot, except as a last resort. First, he tries to fix it himself.

WARNING: Do not try to repair your chainsaw yourself, unless you are familiar with gas engines and sharp instruments flying about, and know what you are doing.

The problem with my chainsaw, I quickly deduced, was that the little plastic hose that runs from the gas tank to the thingamajig had come loose. Right away, I guessed that this was the reason the saw was spewing gas all over the place. I slipped the hose back on the doohickey and fastened it down with a glob of acrylic something-or-other I've had on a shelf in the garage aging for the past nine years. So far, I haven't worked up the nerve to pull the starter cord, but sooner or later one of my sons-in-law will be over, and I'll be able to give him a little experience with a chainsaw.

Anyway, I mentioned to my wife, Bun, that I've been thinking about buying another chainsaw. I said, "You know what with the economy being what it is, we might want to put in a good supply of wood from the national forest, enough to last us through the winter, just in case. That way, we would at least be warm, even if we had to huddle around the fireplace."

I should mention here that Bun is not a chainsaw kind of wife. Furthermore, I don't like to hear a woman respond to a serious suggestion with a laugh.

"Haw!" she laughed. "You're not getting another chainsaw until you get rid of the two you already have out in the garage. I stumble over one or the other every time I go out there."

I tried to explain to her that a chainsaw is almost impossible to get rid of. If you're giving it away, the potential recipient already knows it probably doesn't work. The garbage people don't want you sneaking it into your garbage can, and the dump people have no category for chainsaws that are spewing gas all over everything. They view them as threats to the environment. What's a dump for, anyway?

So I'm keeping my chainsaws.

I have been associated with chainsaws all my life, since I was a teenager. Before that, we used a big crosscut saw. Back in those days, you would have a logger friend haul you in a couple of buckskin tamarack logs in the fall, each one slightly smaller than a railroad tank car. After school each day, the kid in the family would go out and saw a block off one of the logs. One block, split up into heater chunks and cookstove pieces, was enough to keep the home fires burning for a day. Sometimes, unless your friends were really smart and wary, one of them would come home with you and help you saw off the block of firewood.

I was only seven or eight the first time I ever sawed with a partner. He complained that I was "riding the saw." That's an expression you don't hear much anymore. Anytime someone wasn't doing his share of the work back then, he was said to be "riding the saw." I heard it a lot. The expression must have been very popular in those days. What it meant was that after you had pulled the saw to your side of the log, you were supposed to relax your arm so that your partner didn't have to pull both you and the saw back. You usually didn't commit this sin until your arms were about to fall off. It wasn't that I didn't know about riding the saw, but simply that I kept forgetting. As a seven-year-old, I had a lot of other things on my mind.

By the time I reached my teens, chainsaws had come along. For a person who had spent his early youth riding the saw, I thought they were one of the greatest inventions of all times. A logger we knew would loan us his chainsaw when he wasn't using it, and my stepfather and I would mow down trees like tall grass and whip them into firewood lengths. The saw was only slightly heavier than a Buick. It had a chain on it that could slice through a log like a knife through butter. Once my stepfather fell on the saw, and we had to take him home in quart jars. No, only kidding. Fortunately, the saw wasn't running at the time of his fall. He did get some really nice scars, but I thought it a rather risky way to get them.

Eventually, we got our own chainsaw, a much smaller model, and it was a marvel. One fall when I was a sophomore in college, I went home for a weekend, and in one afternoon my girlfriend and I cut up enough firewood to last my folks all winter. I zipped through trees and cut them into eight-foot lengths for my girlfriend to load into the back of a pickup. We hauled them home where the two of us finished cutting them up into firewood lengths with a circular power saw. It was amazing that a skinny girl and I could accomplish so much in a single day. I never saw Olga again after that and often wondered what happened to her.

As an adult, I have never been without a chainsaw. Back in the time when Bun and I had young children at home, we would pile all the kids into the family car and tow a trailer up into the mountains to cut our winter's wood. The youngsters loved it. Oh, how I remember their shrill screams as I pried their fingers off the beds and sent them out to get into the car for yet another adventure into the mountains for a load of firewood. It was a fun time.

My friend Retch Sweeney is a chainsaw kind of guy. You might even think of him as a chainsaw addict. He sets the throttle on his saw fairly high, so the chain continues to rotate and pulls the saw along the ground, something Retch calls "saw creep." He says he's thinking of buying a leash and attaching it to the saw so he can walk behind and be pulled up the mountain by it. Retch is what you might call the Ultimate Chainsaw Kind of Guy.

Then, of course, there's Barney Wapshot. He's had his saw a whole week and probably doesn't even know the words you use to get a chainsaw started. Maybe I'll go over and teach them to him. The economy being what it is, I might have to borrow his saw someday.

The Lady Who Kept Things

There was once a small, plump, good-natured lady who lived in a great, old house with her cantankerous husband, Harold. She was about the best mate a man could have, and he was about the worst mate anyone could have.

The lady, whose name was Emma, had a peculiar habit, however, which was that she never threw anything away. Her closets bulged with heaps of clothes, and stacks of magazines, and balls of string, and boxes of buttons—in short, just about everything that had ever entered into the life of Emma was still there someplace, boxed or bundled up in the great, old house.

Now this eccentricity grated on Harold's nerves like a rasp on glass, so he used it as a convenient excuse to take up with a platinum blonde who bought peroxide at his drugstore. The friendship flourished into an affair, and soon Harold was away on business trips almost every weekend. In fact, business became so good that he was often called away in the middle of the week, and Emma began to think she had married a traveling salesman instead of a druggist.

But she was good-natured, innocent, and never suspected anything amiss. She spent her lonely evening boxing and bundling things that had come into her daily life, and chatted happily away with her beloved pets—a Scottie dog named Jack, a cat, a canary, and seven goldfish with no names whatsoever.

Harold was a simple man by nature, and after a while he decided that his modern way of life was setting too fast a pace for him and had become too complicated. One of his women would have to go, and it wasn't going to be the blonde, even though she couldn't cook.

He didn't want to kill Emma. This wasn't because he was sentimental, but rather because he was squeamish and had a weak stomach. Besides, he had long toyed with the idea of whether it was possible to drive a person to insanity. If anyone could do it, Harold was sure he could.

Emma had quite a little money, which, naturally, she kept, and Harold wanted to be sure the money would be placed under his supervision when Emma went off the deep end. He would need the extra cash for two fares to Bermuda.

Harold started off his project by instilling in Emma's mind doubts about herself. She wouldn't be able to find one of her shoes; it would turn up in a pan with a lid on it inside the oven. He hooked up a special switch into the electrical wiring so he could control the light in her bedroom. She would turn off the light, go to sleep, and when she awoke in the night the light would be on.

Harold had half a dozen such plots and devices going simultaneously and continuously. But about the only effect his scheme had on Emma was that her saving instinct had taken on a new intensity. She had actually begun to save the scraps of food from the dinner table, sealing them up tight in quart jars. Now, although this should have been an encouraging sign, the more she saved the more pleasant and calm she became.

Harold knew that if his plan were to succeed in a reasonable amount of time, he would have to deal a shattering blow to his wife's joviality.

This brought about the weird incident with the dog, Jack.

One evening, Harold brought home from his drugstore some arsenic powder and stored it in the medicine cabinet. The next morning, Jack ate breakfast in his usual hurried fashion, rolled over on his back, and passed away. Emma was stricken with sadness at the loss of her pet. No longer was the light of joy in her eyes, and she sat in her chair in the great, old house—the dark and dusty and crammed-full house—and rocked the dead dog Jack back and forth, back and forth in the living room.

Harold smiled to himself as he went out the door for a three-day trip, but it was an uneasy smile that hung faint and timid on his lips.

Returning home later in the week, he stepped nonchalantly into the living room and leaped halfway to the top of a stack of old catalogs, sending a box of empty ink bottles clattering to the floor.

"What in hell is that?" he screamed at his wife.

"Jack," she said.

"Jack!" he yelled, the hair lifting on the back of his neck.

"Yes," she said. "I had him stuffed."

It took Harold several days to grow accustomed to the glassy and accusing stare of Jack, but he knew he must hurry if he were to take advantage of his wife's low spirits, which had already picked up remarkably and were almost back to their normal jovial state.

It was the cat's turn next to play its role in Harold's little drama. The cat ate its breakfast, looked disturbed, and died. Harold went off on a trip. When he came back, he didn't flick an eyelash at the cat curled rather stiffly in its usual place in front of the hearth. But an almost imperceptible chill, like an ant with cold feet, crawled up his back.

Next came the canary. One day it was dead, and the next it was back in its cage, still and silent on its perch. And, worst of all, the death of the bird seemed to have absolutely no effect on Emma.

The stuffed menagerie, however, was beginning to make Harold nervous, and he felt a powerful urge for haste in his weird task, and a yearning for well-lighted and distant places where people kept nothing at all.

And then it happened. The goldfish were waiting belly up in their bowl one morning when Harold came down for breakfast, and this was strange indeed, for he hadn't poisoned the goldfish!

While he sipped his coffee and contemplated this turn of events, Emma bustled here and there about the kitchen. She scooped the goldfish from their bowl with a tea strainer and hurried across the room to a cabinet that was stacked with the usual conglomeration of bottles, glasses, and vats, most of which contained some preserved and cherished perishable that had entered into the life of Emma.

"What in hell do you think you're doing?" Harold said in his usual dull and acid voice. He sipped his coffee.

"Pickling my goldfish," she said happily. "Yes, pickling my goldfish. It would be so terribly sad to bury them in the ground and never see them again, never, never again, until the world stops and all is lost forever."

Harold looked at Emma keenly. Could it really be? He poured himself another cup of coffee, which tasted terrible this morning, but he hardly noticed. Could it be that all this time his wife had actually been insane, and he hadn't noticed it? She had been off her rocker all along. Why, it was so obvious now. No sane person would keep things the way she did. He watched her hurry to the other side of the room, and he smiled. Perhaps he would start proceedings for her commitment to an asylum that very morning. Well, maybe he would wait until the afternoon, because he really wasn't feeling too well.

He sipped his coffee. Emma was going briskly about her task across the room. She had finished pickling the fish. He watched her and forced himself to smile, despite the hot glow in his stomach. Bermuda, he thought. I'll leave tomorrow. His neck felt rather stiff this morning, and the hot Bermuda sun would be good for it. He sipped his coffee, but his hand shook, and he sloshed coffee on the table. Harold stopped smiling, and he wondered how long it would take for the world to end, and what would become of all the long-lost things when the end came. And he slipped forward onto the table now, and thought somberly about the dog, Jack, and the cat, and canary, and the seven goldfish. Emma was just a fuzzy silhouette, bustling about her task across the room. She worked briskly, happily humming some queer little tune. Harold watched her and waited.

She was emptying out the deep freeze. It was quite a large deep freeze.

September Song

According to the poet T. S. Eliot, April is the cruelest month. I have never found April to be particularly cruel. For me, at least, as a youth, September was the cruelest month. After a summer of running wild and free, suddenly I found myself confined in school. During the latter days of August, I had somehow beguiled myself into thinking school might be fun that year, even though I had no evidence on which to base this theory.

Certainly our teachers did not regard their jobs as intended to keep their youthful charges entertained. After the first hour of listening to our English teacher go on and on about the horrors of dangling participles, which, as I recall, turned out to be some kind of South American tree lizard and better left to the biology teacher, I realized I had been seriously mistaken about school being fun. The thought of nine months of this tedium was almost more than I could bear. Only one thing preserved my September sanity: grouse season!

Every year, grouse season opened the first of September, the only hunting opportunity since the previous November when my stepfather and I ventured out on Thanksgiving Day in our annual quest of a winter's supply of venison. My recollection, enhanced by half a century and more, is that obtaining said supply of protein consisted of little more than going out in the woods and standing around for an hour or so until a deer showed up. It was not exactly the kind of hunting I had read about in the outdoor magazines, which consisted of spraying yourself with scent and rattling horns, climbing a tree to a deer stand, and that sort of thing. Grouse season, on the other hand, was real hunting. My friend Norman and I may have missed a day of hunting grouse during those distant cruel Septembers, but if we did, I cannot recall it.

Norman and I would plan each evening's hunt during our ride home on the school bus, which actually wasn't a great place to plan anything. Two of the smaller kids would get into a fight and be thrashing around on the floor and some of the older kids would be egging them on, and finally Ed Schramm, the bus driver, would stop the bus, come back down the aisle, grab each of the fighters by the nape of the neck, hold them up in the air kicking and screaming, and say to me and Norman, "Where you boys hunting tonight?"

We would reply, "Probably this side of Sand Crick, Ed."

He would be holding the two fighters out at arm's length and say, "Well, I hit that side pretty hard last night and didn't see much of anything. I'd try the other side, if I was you."

I'd say, "Thanks, Ed, we'll probably do that." Then Ed would haul the two screaming brats to the front of the bus and toss them out the door. As I say, the school bus wasn't the best place in the world to plan a hunt, but Ed was always willing to help out if he could.

Norman got off the bus about a mile before my place, so he always got a jump on our hunt by half an hour or so. He hunted with a single shot his folks had bought for him brand-new out of a mail-order catalog for about $8. Norman said he preferred that model of shotgun over all the other models, possibly because it could mow down trees and maybe even a barn, if it got in the way. It sounded like a cannon when it went off, and Norman's eyeballs would pop out about half an inch from the recoil. He almost never missed a grouse, but sometimes about all we could find of it was feathers, some of them still drifting down out of the air.

When it came to my gun, I had to make do with a hand-me-down. My mother had married a Frenchman a few years back, and while he was trying to get on my better side, he gave me a French-made side-by-side with engraved barrels and a carved stock. It had been handed down to him by his father, who had immigrated from France. The gun worked all right even if it didn't come mail-order, and I was happy to have any gun at all, even a French one. One thing I'll say about Norman, he never put on airs about having a mail-order gun and one that could mow down trees with a single shot and sounded like a cannon when it went off.

After I got off the bus, I would run all the way down to our big old farmhouse, bang through the front door, grab my gun and a pocket full of shells, scoop up a hot cinnamon roll from a batch my grandmother had just dumped out to cool on the kitchen table, then go out the back door and jump from the porch to the ground with Gram coming out behind me waving a butcher knife as I fled across the back pasture, headed for the crick.

I crossed the crick on a beaver dam. Crossing cricks on beaver dams was an art form in those days, and if you were good at it, you could make it across without getting a foot wet, even while munching a hot cinnamon roll, a hunting technique all but forgotten nowadays.

Those September grouse hunts were all glorious, but one in particular stands out. It provided one of those moments in time that never fade from memory. Norman and I met up half a mile or so down crick and were moseying along a side hill when we came upon Rancid Crabtree, a rank old woodsman who lived in a little cabin back against the mountain.

Indeed, we could smell him before we caught sight of him, although this wasn't particularly unusual.

"By golly," Norman said, "I think we're downwind of Rancid."

Rancid was in a rage when we got to him. He was holding his shotgun in two pieces, the stock in one hand and the barrel in the other. He seemed glad to see us, apparently so that his ranting would at least have an appreciative audience.

"What happen," he said, sitting down on a nearby log, "me and Wuff was comin' down that steep trail from the Walkers' farm when we come to a skonk. Now you boys know how much ah hates skonks. Wahl, Wuff hates 'em twice as much. Fust thank ah knows, he's tearin' after the skonk. Thet skonk, though, is a sly, old fellar and wiggles his way into a patch of brush. The brush slows Wuff down and finally stops him cold. The skonk is now firin' at him point-blank. Ah would of blasted it, but ah was a feared of hittin' Wuff, so ah wades into the brush and now the skonk had got me in its range and ah'm almost blinded, but ah swings maw shotgun at the critter. Jist than ah steps into a patch of wet clay from thet spring up the hill, go down flat on maw belly, and whacks a log with maw gun. Broke it in two pieces. The skonk wiggles off scot-free, but him and me is gonna meet up agin, ah kin tell you thet! Iffin ah could of got maw hands on him, ah would've choked him to death."

"Gosh, Rance," Norman said, "I think a skunk would be about the worst thing in the world for a person to choke."

"Yer right about thet, Norman! Ah guess it depends how mad the skonk makes you in the first place. Chokin' a skonk ain't somethin' you spend any time thankin' about, thet's fer dang shore."

Having had considerable experience with skunks, I tried to give Rancid some advice. "I got sprayed by a skunk last summer, Rance, and my mother made me sit in a tub of boiling water while she poured a whole gallon of vinegar over me. You should give it a try."

"Maybe ah will. On t'other hand, thar ain't no point in bein' hasty about a thang like thet. If the smell don't wear off by spring, ah'll thank about tryin' what you said, Patrick."

It was from this experience with Rancid that Norman and I learned the importance of the terms "upwind" and "downwind." We found this bit of wisdom a whole lot more valuable than learning about some stupid South American tree lizard.

The Longest March

I slumped in my office chair, desperately trying to think of an opening for a story about the horrors of March.

"March is longer than a supper of boiled liver."

Naw, that won't work.

"God made March just in case eternity proved too brief."

Now that's pretty darn good! Has a Shakespearean quality to it, a bit of class.

"March is the *plop-plop* without the *fizz-fizz*."

Scratch that.

How does the old saying go—if March comes in like a lion, it will go out like a lamb? Personally, I always thought of March as coming in like a dead toad and going out like a dead toad.

That pretty well captures my feelings about March. On the other hand, the Friends of Toads might get after me for bad-mouthing their amphibian.

"If the year has an embarrassing itch, March would be the place to scratch."

Did I want to risk another letter from the lady in Ohio complaining about my depravity? No, better not.

My wife entered the room we laughingly call my office. "I wish you wouldn't just sit there staring vacantly out the window. What you need is a good hobby!"

"Staring vacantly out the window *is* my March hobby."

Bun has only one bad habit—positive thinking. With all the really fun bad habits around, my wife picks positive thinking.

"What I came to tell you," she said, "is that your youngest daughter wants to know if she can go out on a date with Charlie Harper?"

Ah, young Charlie Harper! Handsome, athletic, polite, a lad of friendly smile and twinkling eyes, he reminded me of myself as a youth. I remembered how I would stand in front of a mirror working on my friendly smile and trying to make my eyes twinkle. "Absolutely not," I shouted. "He's a total fraud. She's not going out with a wild kid like that! I know his kind. He doesn't fool me for a minute."

I hate disruptions. Slowly I forced myself back into reminiscence. It was still March but a different March, the longest March I would ever know. I was sixteen, up in my room in our old farmhouse working on my hobby of staring vacantly off into space. March had already stretched to the edge of time and back, with enough left over to knit a couple of ice ages. I was sick of March and knew that the only thing that could cure me was May and the opening of trout season. For temporary relief, however, I thought how my first cast would unfurl over the swirling waters of Sand Creek, how my worm and sinkers would caress the water with a soft *plop*, be sucked beneath the current and drift into the deep hole beneath the big old black cedar stump to the waiting jaws of a . . .

My name cracked in my ears like a rifle shot. Mom was beckoning me downstairs, her voice strained with urgency. Knowing full well the general portent of my mother's urgent tones, I descended the stairs at a pace commonly associated with snails.

"Yeah?"

"Reverend Twill is here," Mom said. "He needs someone to guide him up to Rancid Crabtree's cabin. Mr. Crabtree may be dying."

I knew Rancid was supposed to be dying. Nobody needed to tell me that. Rancid had been my friend for a long time. Hunter, trapper, angler, rover, philosopher, Rancid was the sort of man who should live forever! Rancid had said so himself. But now he was dying. I wondered what business a preacher could have with the old woodsman.

"What do you want with Rancid?" I asked.

"It's just the business I'm in," said the minister. "I heard Mr. Crabtree was very ill, and I thought I might encourage him to repent of his sins."

I wanted no part of this undertaking. I knew for a fact that Rancid never thought of himself as sinning but rather just having a good time. Not that Rancid didn't, in fact, sin. Indeed, just the previous spring I had heard Rancid sin loudly and at great length when a huge cutthroat snapped his leader. I had never thought it my business, however, to explain sin to a grown man.

"Gosh, I'd like to help you out, Reverend Twill," I said "but there's some important business I got to take care of today." My mother gave me one of her looks.

Bouncing along in the car with Twill, I pondered Mom's explanation of why I should guide the preacher to Rancid's cabin. It was her sound reasoning that persuaded me, its essence condensed to the phrase "Or else!"

Her "or else" covered such a wide range of my privileges that I didn't think I should run the risk of refusing to guide Twill on his mission. Rancid was the happiest person I knew, possibly because he had managed to avoid any serious kind of work his entire life. God wouldn't hold happiness against a person. Rancid even made me happy, which was quite an accomplishment, considering that I lived as the sole male in a house full of prissy women, my mother, my grandmother, and my sister, the Troll.

The preacher's car bucked and twisted in the March mud until it turned off on a track that led through the woods to Rancid's cabin.

"Good heavens! Are you sure, Patrick, this is the way to Crabtree's place?"

"Yeah," I said. "It gets like this most every March. We're coming to the bad part, though."

"The bad part!"

"Henry Porter lost his horse in there last year. Just up and vanished."

Reverend Twill hit the brakes. "Vanished? The horse completely vanished?"

"Yeah. The bad part: Henry was riding it at the time."

"They both vanished?"

I was just beginning to get the story wound up, when the reverend swung the car around in a sharp arc and headed back toward our place.

"That's the worse road I've ever seen!" he shouted.

Actually, it was only a game trail, or had been, since the game had given up using it in favor of the road.

The Reverend Twill dropped me off at my place and headed back to town, where the sinners were more plentiful and easier to save.

A couple days later, I walked through the woods to Rancid's cabin. The sun was out, it was now April, and the old woodsman was sitting on his porch sipping from a jug of whiskey. He was obvious not only still alive but the picture of health.

After I reported the news to him, he shouted, "The preacher was comin' out to see me?" he asked. "What in tarnation he want to do thet fer?"

"Beats me," I said. "Actually, I was kind of disappointed when he turned back because I wanted to hear your sins myself. You could tell them to me now, if you wanted to. I'd forgive you."

Rancid stared at me. "I bet you would."

The Stalk

My friend Retch Sweeney sent me an email last fall detailing a stalk he had just made on a large, gray log bedded down in a grove of young firs. Retch was bow hunting, so it was necessary that he move in relatively close in order to get a shot. At the moment he sighted the log, he was still upwind of it, but the log hadn't detected him yet. He crouched down and swung far out to one side of the log, maneuvering so he could approach from downwind. He soon was within range without the log having detected his approach.

It was at this point that Retch noticed the log was a log and not the resting deer he had first thought. Still, he was proud of the skill with which he had stalked the log and was pretty sure that if it had been a deer, it would have ended up in his freezer.

Retch's stalk reminded me of the time I was leading three friends on an early morning hunt. We were all teenagers, although I can't remember exactly how old. My friends were lined up behind me, all of us tramping silently along in the snow. Usually, I wasn't allowed to lead on our hunts, or on other adventures either, but for some reason that responsibility fell to me on this occasion. Perhaps it was because the morning was beastly cold and it still wasn't light enough to shoot. Maybe no one expected any activity in the immediate future—who knows?

As we moved uphill, I glanced around some bushes and saw a herd of snags moving over the ridge and coming downhill directly at us. I gave a hand signal for everybody to squat down behind the bushes. Time passed slowly. The cold became more intense. Occasionally, I would hear an anguished groan from behind me as the chill of the morning sank into young bones cramped in a tense crouch. My hope was that by the time the herd reached us, there would be enough light for us to shoot. Then it occurred to me the snags might be approaching around the other end of the row of brush. I had the whole group follow me in a duck walk to the other end of the brush. Had the snags possessed hearing, they might easily have detected our heavy breathing, groans, and chattering teeth.

A half-hour oozed by as my frozen ears strained to hear the approach of the snags. The guys had their gloves off, blowing on their frozen trigger fingers. I raised my hand for silence. Then I slowly got up so I could peer over the bushes enough to locate the quarry. That's when I made out that the herd of snags was the same line of snags that had been there for the last hundred years or so. In the early morning light, enhanced by a hunter's expectation, the snags had looked exactly like a herd of mule deer approaching us in single-file. I mean it!

"Dang!" I said, standing up. "They must have cut back over the ridge." This quick thinking probably saved me from a severe beating from my frozen friends. I'm not sure if they suspected anything. On the other hand, I never got to lead again.

Another such stalking experience occurred when I was ten or so. This time, I was the one being stalked. It was the middle of January, and we had been released from school because it was too dangerous for the town kids to walk through the blizzard or for us country kids to wait for the school bus. We greatly appreciated this thoughtfulness on the part of the principal because blizzards could be dangerous in our part of the country. On this particular blizzard day, as we referred to such days, I was returning to my house from several hours of skiing with my friend Vern Schulze. I lived about a quarter of a mile from Vern and was crossing a large field in front of our house when I noticed a large pack of animals prowling back and forth between me and my house.

I hunkered down in the snow so they couldn't see me. The animals continued to pace. Even though I couldn't see them clearly, I was fairly certain they were wolves, probably waiting for me to return home. Somehow they had picked up my scent, probably not that difficult to do, and knew I was in the vicinity. The wolves moved back and forth in a determined fashion, the blowing snow all but concealing the rascals. I made a snowball and threw it at them, but the snow was dry and fluffy and had no effect. In any case, the wolves didn't seem to notice.

I soon began to feel frostbite setting in, and it finally occurred to me that I might as well be eaten by wolves as freeze to death. I got up and started walking toward them. It was then that I began to make out a pile of logs protruding from a drift of snow, the same logs that had been there for a year or more. The wolves had vanished. They hadn't even left tracks, but, of course, the tracks would have been covered by the blowing snow. This goes to show once again how my keen woodsman skills saved me from possible disaster.

All my experience with stalking as a youngster helped shape my approach to other aspects of life as I grew older. It has been my observation over the years, for example, that the most successful hunters are those persons who focus upon their quarry with intense concentration. It was with this particular kind of concentration that I began to stalk a girl during my senior year in high school. Since a variety of creepos have given "stalking" a bad name, I will, in this instance, use the word "pursuing."

As with wild game, the pursuit of a girl requires that you first become aware of your particular quarry. In hunting, you can't wander about in pursuit of whatever comes along—an elk, a rabbit, a grouse, or whatever. If you hope for any success, you have to keep totally focused on the particular game. The same applies to the pursuit of a girl. You must have the particular quarry singled out.

One day, my friend Retch Sweeney showed me a photograph of his cousin. I said instantly, "Wow! I'm going to marry this girl!"

Recovering from a painful fit of mirth, Retch said, "Ha! She's beautiful, smart, and rich. She's only seventeen and already in college, whereas you are—well, you!"

It was true. I was still only a high school senior, poor, with bad hair, bad eyesight, and mediocre grades. I never wore my glasses at school. Anything occurring up near the blackboard was a mystery to me. The only time I wore my glasses was when I was out hunting, and then largely at the insistence of my hunting companions.

My only attribute in those days was my enormous self-confidence. Nothing in my life provided any reason for this peculiar characteristic, and for some unknown reason I felt certain I could achieve whatever I set my mind to—in this instance, a particular girl.

She was a Montana girl, by the way, and I highly recommend Montana girls as prospective wives of outdoorsmen. They are hard on the outside and soft on the inside. But my mother-in-law was also a Montana girl, and she was hard on the outside and hard on the inside, so you do have to be careful of Montana girls.

I possessed the same intensity in pursuing this girl that I did in the pursuit of wild game. Often I'd place myself on stand near someplace I thought she might be passing by. "Oh, hi," I would say. "Fancy meeting you here."

"We live in that house."

"Ah, that explains it. Would you like to go for a Coke?"

"No."

As with hunting, you can't be discouraged when the quarry eludes you. The successful hunter needs to learn as as much as possible about his quarry. I used my friend Retch as a research resource.

"Does she like pleasing aromas?" I asked.

"I suppose."

"Maybe she would respond to a particular scent."

"I wouldn't describe your scent as a pleasing aroma."

"I was thinking of something along the lines of aftershave lotion."

"Might work. That and a shower."

I slopped on some of my stepfather's aftershave lotion, but it had no effect on the girl, although it did bring a nice mule deer buck within easy range. The way it kept flaring its nostrils made me nervous, though, and I missed the shot.

Once I even tried camouflage. I borrowed one of my stepfather's dark suits and a tie, and even if I do say so myself, I looked pretty darn debonair. Unfortunately, my stepfather's legs were several inches shorter than mine. Maybe I should have worn some black socks or even painted my ankles with shoe polish.

As with hunting, though, persistence paid off. It took several years, but I eventually married the girl. Her previous boyfriend reportedly said he wouldn't have minded so much if I hadn't been so funny-looking. Ha! Talk about somebody who needed glasses!

The Horse in My Garage

O ver the years, my wife and I have successfully managed to indenture ourselves to the usual number and variety of pets that the average child needs to sustain life. As any parent knows, these creatures range in size from a few ounces to half a ton (and if one steps on your foot, you may be sure it won't be the one weighing a few ounces).

The portion of suburban sprawl we called home was still zoned for agriculture, an oversight on the part of the county planning committee that allowed us to keep a pet horse on our one-acre spread, which stretches off as far as the eye can see, depending on the air pollution on any particular day. Sooner or later, the planning commission would zone us into urbanity, and we would have to get rid of the horse—the sooner the better, in my opinion.

Since we had no barn, the horse, whose name was Huckleberry, resided in my garage. My automobile resided in the driveway, in a spot apparently under the holding pattern of a large flock of pigeons—a species of bird apparently not all that good at holding. Not only was I embarrassed to be seen driving a vehicle that looked as if it had been used in a scientific study in pigeon irregularity, but I was tired of having a horse in my garage. It might be inferred from this diatribe that I was a person who isn't fond of horses. That is wrong. I detest horses.

Why, you ask, would a person who detests horses buy one? You apparently are not the permissive parent of four young children who absolutely love horses. Also, I was probably suffering from temporary impairment of judgment at the time I made the purchase. The cowboy who sold us the horse made a great show of petting and stroking the beast, apparently to show me how gentle it was. Later, I concluded that he was simply wiping off his fingerprints.

I learned a great deal about horses over the many years we owned Huckleberry. For example, the basic diet of horses is hay, which you may think of as simply long grass that sensible folks keep mowed close to the ground. Upon going to the feed store for a few bales, however, you discover from the price that it is a rare plant hand-picked on the other side of the world and flown first-class to the feed store. Horses also eat large quantities of oats, a substance smuggled into the country under the dashboards of luxury automobiles. Occasionally, the horse will take for dessert a bucketful of small green pellets compressed from shredded $5 bills. The horse will also seek out a poisonous weed and eat it, for no other reason than his enjoyment in a trip to the vet's. Although our vet has never told me, I suspect he was formerly a brain surgeon who gave up that profession in favor of one where there was real money to be made.

Oh, I almost forgot. Horses also need shoes. I had never expected Huckleberry to provide me with entertainment, but at the time of his purchase I didn't know anyone who made an occupation of putting metal shoes on horses. Because the process took place behind my garage, I never observed it firsthand. The sound effects, however, were wonderful, including such classics as, "Git off my foot, you bleeping bleep of a bleep!"

This would be screamed at a pitch so high it was almost impossible to comprehend. The amusement provided by the old horseshoer was almost worth the cost. If you figure in how much he improved my vocabulary, his service was almost priceless. I think the horse enjoyed the process almost as much as I did.

I have to admit that Huck turned out to be a wonderful horse for children, very seldom taking a bite out of one of them and usually in a place where it wouldn't show. If the youngest child was put on his back, he would plod along like a creature suffering cardiac arrest. Somehow, Huck managed to judge how much riding experience each rider possessed and adjusted his pace to fit. As he grew older, his docility seemed to increase. Observing this, one day I decided to go for a ride myself.

"Guess what," I said to my wife, Bun, in the kitchen one day. "I think I'll go out and ride Old Huck."

"Are you crazy!" she exclaimed. "You don't know anything about horses."

"You may be surprised to learn this," I said, "but for many years I nursed an ambition to be a cowboy. Now go hunt down that steel thing you put in his mouth, and the leather straps you use to steer him with. Then I'll show you how much I know about horses."

Together we herded Huck up against a board fence and gave him a bucket of oats to munch in preparation for my climbing aboard, as we cowboys say. I had thought about putting the saddle on his back but that seemed a bit of a nuisance, since I planned to ride him no further than the other end of the pasture and back, an area about the size of a football field. Huck appeared to be half-asleep. Finishing off the contents of the bucket, he lifted his head and looked around. He then clamped his jaws tentatively around my wrist, apparently in an effort to prevent me from putting the steel thing in his mouth. Putting the steel thing into a horse's mouth, by the way, frequently brings on sustained fits of gagging, so for several hours before undertaking the task, it is best not to eat anything. I grabbed the steering lines, climbed the corral fence, and leaped on Huck's bare back.

"Wait!" Bun cried anxiously, "Aren't you going to put on the blanket and saddle?"

"Naw," I replied. "I'll just ride him naked."

For those who may be unacquainted with the nuances of horsemanship, I should explain that riding a naked horse is much more difficult than riding one equipped with a saddle and blanket. I intended a brief ride, however, and in that case, a blanket and saddle are more of a hindrance than a help, or so I thought at the time.

What prompted Huckleberry's sudden and unprovoked display of athleticism, I will never know. As I was settling myself on his barren back, my legs splayed out over his barrel belly, the beast took off like Man o' War out of the starting gate. We roared across the front yard, around the back of the house, jumped a plastic wading pool, and pounded full throttle down the pasture, myself now crouched like a monkey on his back, and still roaring, "Whoa! Whoa! You . . . !" Here I inserted some of the colorful words I had picked up from the old man who put the metal shoes on the creature. The words had no effect, as I should have judged from having listened to the old man.

Suddenly, I remembered the steering lines. I let go of Huck's mane, grabbed the lines, and hauled back on them. My effort had no effect. There was too much slack in them. The galloping had vibrated me forward! I was now bouncing up and down on the large bony bump that connects a horse's neck to the rest of him. There was only one thing to do. I threw myself forward and grabbed the horse around the neck. Perhaps I thought I could choke him into stopping, I don't know.

We were now at the far end of the pasture, the fence between us and a busy road that we were approaching at incredible speed. For a moment, I thought Huck was planning to jump the fence, but at the last moment he made a right-angle turn at full throttle, something I later learned that quarter horses are trained to do. Actually, I don't know if they are trained to cut sharp corners at high speed, or just make it up on their own, as a method of displacing cowboys. Whatever. In any case, the movement swept me around under the horse's neck, his pounding front hooves now but inches away. He had not slowed his pace in the slightest. I somehow managed to get my legs clasped above his neck next to my clasped hands. Huck made another right-hand turn, perhaps thinking he could finish dislodging me in that manner, and headed back down the pasture. He slid to a stop right in front of Bun. I peered at her upside-down. She stood there as if frozen to the spot, mouth agape, eyes stricken.

I unclasped my legs and swung to the ground. "What would you like to see now?" I said, turning to her. One thing about us cowboys, we know how to be cool in front of the ladies.

The Tent

Some people are born brave. I am not one of them. During the summers I was twelve and thirteen, I started camping out a mile or so up a little creek that tumbled down out of a narrow canyon a couple hours hike from my house. I didn't camp out alone, of course. I wasn't crazy. Usually there were four of us, Reggie, Ernie, Herbie, and me. Reggie was our leader because he was tall, athletic, and had good hair. And he was brave.

We all had a great deal of experience sleeping out from the time we were very young. But there is a big difference between sleeping out and camping out. Sleeping out is done in your backyard. Camping out is done off in the woods or mountains, well beyond the range of suddenly running into your house, as often happened with sleeping out. The difference between sleeping out and camping out was primarily one of distance.

While sleeping out, a sudden retreat into the house was usually ignited by the amount of darkness in the world. You would be lying there in your sleeping bag looking up at the sky, the whole world filled with darkness, and suddenly the sheer vastness of the dark overpowered you. Many people who haven't slept out don't know that, but it's true. Dark becomes an irresistible force, and your senses go on red alert. An ant tramping by or a mosquito's cough could ignite a sudden retreat, but usually the alarm wasn't so major.

I should point out that no one actually slept while sleeping out. No matter how slight the sound, it would trigger some mechanism in your legs, and the next moment you would be hurtling through the back door of your house, your sleeping bag or blankets still fluttering to the ground.

Camping out, on the other hand, left you imprisoned out in the wild, with great blocks of dark between you and your back door. Sometimes you would actually fall asleep while camping out, but usually not until the second or third night. I can still recall the wonderful relief of waking up the next morning still alive and in one piece. There is no more glorious sight to young campers than the first sliver of sun rising over a distant mountain.

One summer, Ernie's parents came up with a brilliant solution to the dark. They bought him a little, white canvas tent. If the four of us slept side-by-side in it, no farther apart than bread slices in a packaged loaf, we fit nicely. I don't remember if the tent was waterproof or if it kept the rain out, but it did keep most of the dark out. Being a small tent, it limited the dark to a few cubic feet, a couple dozen at most, but it established a limit. You no longer had the sense that the whole world was filled with dark. True, I did realize a grizzly could chomp down the whole tent and us as if we were nothing more than a bear-size taco, but grizzlies were nothing compared with limitless dark.

Right here, I should mention that Reggie had a serious fault as a camping companion—he was fearless. One of us regular guys would hiss something like, "I just heard something!"

Reggie would say, "It ain't nothin'! Shut up and go to sleep!"

I wanted so much to be like Reggie, to be brave and calm while camping out, and to actually sleep.

This brings me to the night Reggie got up and left the tent to answer a call of nature. I know this sounds crazy to any former kid campers, but it's true. That's how fearless Reggie was. He thought nothing of getting up in the middle of the night and going outside the tent. Nature could have been shrieking in one of my ears and often was, and I would not have budged toward the limitless dark. I was so comfortable in the embrace of that little tent that I never even noticed Reggie's foolhardy act and may even have drifted off to sleep.

The next morning, Reggie insisted on relating his adventure to the rest of us. He told us how he had been standing alongside the tent during the night answering the call, and the moon was out, and he was listening to all the little night sounds and enjoying the moment when suddenly a huge bear ambled by on the other side of the creek. At that point, the creek was so narrow that the bear could have hopped across it without wetting a paw. I was so overwhelmed by Reggie's report of his own nonchalance in regard to the bear as if it were something he experienced almost every day, his standing out there in the moonlight, calmly watching this huge, carnivorous beast lumber by. I was so envious I could hardly speak. Suddenly Ernie let out a yelp. "Hey! Who peed all over the side of my tent!"

After that, I found myself much more comfortable, camping out with Reggie. He suddenly seemed a lot more like one of us regular guys.

To Smoke a Steelhead

After having been a steelhead fisherman for more than forty years, I recently confessed this aberration to my doctor. He said as deplorable and incurable as this condition might be, he didn't think it would make me dangerous to myself or others and certainly not to steelhead. He himself is a chukar hunter, mostly on the steep breaks of the Snake River. So he should talk.

The point of this essay is simply to provide instructions on how to smoke a steelhead. It is a step-by-step procedure based on my own recent experience of smoking a couple of large steelhead.

The steelhead is a sea-run trout, as you probably know, an actual fish, although many anglers believe it to be a mythical creature, a cruel joke played on them by their friends and enemies to get them out on an icy river at the crack of dawn. There are fiends who will actually do this, and the rotten, no-good . . . but I don't want to get carried away. Dedicated fishermen might go through a lifetime without hooking a single steelhead. It is, however, quite easy to pretend that you have caught numerous large steelhead, but that is a topic for another how-to piece.

For the purpose of this lesson, I will use my own experience of smoking my two steelhead. (I have witnesses to the catching, although I would not believe any of them myself.)

First, let me explain that most of my life I have been interested in preserving food by the process of smoking. As a child, I could never understand why my folks insisted upon preserving our own home-raised pork with curing salt rather than build a smokehouse. I can still remember rubbing curing salt into slabs of bacon. If my recollection is correct, my hands were better preserved than the bacon. My folks didn't seem to mind eating deteriorating bacon around March or April, but what could you expect from persons who made and ate homemade blood sausage and headcheese? Homemade headcheese always reminds me that there is such a thing as evil in the world. My family could gross out the average civilized diner at a hundred yards.

Eventually, at about age thirty-five, I finally made enough money to buy a hovel of my own and move my little family into it. It was sort of a small, suburban farm on which I thought we might be able to become self-sustaining by growing our own food and such. (Writers have such weird ideas.) One of my first tasks was to build, at long last, my own smokehouse. It was about two feet square and six feet high, and made of used cedar boards. I drilled a hole in the door and inserted the long proboscis of a meat thermometer through the hole, so I could keep track of the temperature inside. About six feet away, I dug a hole in the ground and lined it with bricks. I ran a sewer pipe underground from the hole over to the smokehouse. (I recommend that if you build your own smokehouse of this design, you buy a new section of sewer pipe.)

Thus I could build a fire in the hole with, say applewood or alder, and the smoke would cool as it flowed through the sewer pipe to the smokehouse. I could control the temperature by sliding a large flat rock back and forth over the fire hole. It was a very nice setup, except for the fact that visitors often mistook the smokehouse for a privy. This can be a real downer, especially for a person who loves his smokehouse.

I smoked all kinds of things in my smokehouse. For example, I once made antelope sausage, stuffing it in casings my wife, Bun, sewed from muslin. Even though the smoked links in no way resembled an antelope, my young daughters, still enamored of Bambi, refused to eat them.

Another time, I smoked some carp and took it to a party. I explained that it was salmon. The guests loved it, including two airline stewardesses who gorged themselves on the "salmon" to the extent that they became quite ill and were out in the yard . . . well, I won't go into that. They no doubt would have been much sicker if I had told them they had been eating carp.

Perhaps the most startling of my smoked creations was a turkey. I had forgotten to tie down its wing and legs, and it came out looking like a fat, brown Superman preparing to leap from a tall building. After laughing themselves sick, the girls refused to eat any of it.

For all these years then, I have been smoking various foods—mostly fish—but occasionally jerky. I once took some of my smoked jerky on a backpacking trip with a professor friend of mine, who referred to the gnarled little black pieces as resembling something that might be found in the vicinity of a small camel. He nevertheless ate a considerable quantity.

I should point out that I no longer use a smokehouse but a product called Little Chief. I don't usually name products, but as I view the Little Chief as one of the greatest inventions in the whole history of the civilized world, I do so here. Now at last, here is how to smoke a steelhead, with detailed instructions based on my own recent experience.

First, you go out to your garage and lay a sheet of plywood or perhaps an old door across two sawhorses. This will make you an adequate filleting table.

Do not—I repeat, DO NOT—attempt to fillet the steelhead in the kitchen. This can be dangerous to your health. I don't think an explanation is necessary.

Once you have the filleting table set up, take the fish from the cooler in which you transported it home. The fish will be bent in the shape of the letter C. That is because the cooler was too small for the steelhead. In my case, the cooler was very large, but I still had to bend the fish to get it to fit. I had covered the fish with ice obtained from a hotel ice machine. I can't recommend using hotel ice. It has no ill effects on fish but a good deal on hotel managers. Maybe you should go to the store and buy a couple bags of ice.

You might wish to speed up the process of straightening your steelhead. I recommend that you arrange the fish so that the bent part is facing up. Then you place a newspaper over the bent part and place a bag of lead shot on top of the newspaper. It has been many years since I've purchased a bag of lead shot, and I don't know how much it costs now. I would not recommend that you run out at this time and buy shot. It is better to substitute some other object, such as a heavy car jack. This will cut in half the time required to straighten your fish.

Once your fish has straightened out, you can begin the filleting process. First, remove the lead shot or car jack. Then take your fillet knife and—wait, I should say a word about fillet knives. Years ago, I bought a large fillet knife. Its blade is at least eighteen inches long and—in theory, at least—it allows you to slice off a large fillet from each side of your fish in a single graceful motion. The knife was very expensive but worth every dollar. For example, one of my sons-in-law once said to me, "Wow! What do you use a knife like that for?"

I said, "For filleting large steelhead and salmon." See, the knife paid for itself right there.

Alas, in this instance, the knife would not penetrate the skin of the steelhead, and I had to resort to the small knife

I used for cleaning and skinning perch. Once the fillets had been whittled off, I attempted to remove the skin from the fillets. Neither my large knife nor the small one allowed me to slice between the skin and the fillet itself. So I simply cut the fillets into three-inch-square chunks ready to go into the brine. I knew that after smoking, the skin would slip right off. Actually, it's quite a bit of fun, peeling the skin from pieces of smoked steelhead, provided you have a low entertainment threshold.

Once you have your steelhead fillets cut into chunks, just place them in a large bowl and pour two cups each of brown sugar and non-iodized salt over them. Then—well, in my case, I discovered at that point that I had only one cup of brown sugar. So I drove to the store and bought another package. The trip took scarcely more than an hour and $15 in gas. I poured the second cup of brown sugar over the fish and started to add the salt. It was at that point I discovered our salt was iodized. So I drove back to the store for non-iodized salt. This trip took scarcely more than an hour and $20 in gas. (The price of Regular gas had gone up in the meantime.) I poured the salt over the steelhead. This is a very simple method of making brine because salt and sugar will draw the juices out of the fish and provide the curing liquid. Because we usually eat the smoked fish within a day or two, I'm not sure about the degree of curing. You're on your own there.

I like to let the fish remain in the brine for eight hours. Because it was now two in the afternoon, the fish would be ready for the Little Chief by ten in the evening. Because I let it smoke for six hours, this meant by four in the morning my smoked steelhead would be done. I checked the TV guide for late-evening and early-morning shows.

And that's all there is to smoking a steelhead. Well, first you have to catch one. So while you're sitting there on your patio, watching your Little Chief puff sway, you may recall that the last time you were in a fish shop, fillets of smoked salmon were going for $20 a pound! You smile to yourself, knowing that this is your own steelhead you're smoking, the one you caught yourself. Indeed, you chortle out loud, thinking about all the people who choose to take the cheap way out. Ha! A mere $20 a pound! Those pikers!

The Teachings of Rancid Crabtree

The first time Rancid Crabtree came to visit at our farm, my mother called me in to meet the old man. I thought of him as old, even though he probably was no more than forty.

"Mr. Crabtree," Mom said. "This is my son, Patrick."

"How old is it?" Rancid asked, as if considering the purchase of some meat of questionable quality.

"Ten."

"Don't have no dad, you say?"

"No, his father died when Patrick was very young." Both of them looked at me as if I were to blame.

Then Rancid asked me the question that grown men in that time and place used to size up a youngster. "Gotcher deer yet?"

"Sure," I replied, modestly scuffing a black mark in the kitchen linoleum with my tennis shoe. "Got him in the head with my .25/20 at 100 yards, a four-point muley. . . . "

Rancid nodded approvingly. "He might do," he said to my mother.

"Oh, *pshaw*!" Mom said. "He's never even fired a gun, let alone killed a deer. He tells stories like that all the time. Land sakes, he keeps me at my wits end. . . . "

"Yup," Rancid said. "He'll do. Shucks, ah couldn't lie like thet till ah was twice his age. Yup, he'll do. . . . "

Those were the first words of encouragement I had heard in all my ten years. I felt the need to express my gratitude to the old man.

"Dressed out upward of a hundred pounds," I said.

Mom rolled her eyes, but Rancid nodded in appreciation.

Until Rancid came along, I resided in a jungle of apron strings, those of my mother, my sister (the Troll), and my grandmother (Gram). Outnumbered three to one, I had fought diligently against this female conspiracy, whose stated objective was to turn me into a civilized young man, a creature never before seen in our part of the country, at least, to my knowledge. Since none of the conspiracy had ever seen a civilized young man as far as I knew, it was unlikely they would recognize such a thing if they saw one. It became increasingly clear to me that what they were trying to do was turn me into a civilized young lady, and I would have none of it. Still, there was some evidence they might succeed. One day, I even washed my hands before supper without being threatened. I was unnerved for hours afterward. The lapse shook my confidence.

Then Rancid Crabtree blew into my life like a breath of fresh air, although that simile is perhaps inappropriate. Among his other activities, Rancid was a trapper of skunks and other innocent creatures of the forest whose furs were bought by a rather creepy individual who passed through our county two or three times a winter. The story was told of Rancid that he had once done hand-to-hand combat with a live skunk, and the skunk had won, but depending on the direction of the wind, you couldn't tell any difference in him. Up until then, I believe he wasn't known as Rancid but as Clarence Crabtree, or something like that. It never seemed to me that Rancid smelled all that bad except maybe when he got wet on a hot day and you were standing too close to him.

Mostly, to me, Rancid smelled like freedom. He lived in a log cabin he had built himself, off in the woods at the foot of the mountains that reared up behind our farm. Although he would help neighbors with their haying or threshing, he would refuse to take money for his effort. As far as I knew, he had never held an actual job. It was considered impolite to mention the word "work" within his hearing. He told me that one time he had gotten too near an actual job, and it had put him in bed sick for three days, and he had never been that foolish again.

Rancid lived exactly the kind of life I planned for myself, and over the rest of my childhood years I studied him carefully.

In my opinion, Rancid knew everything worth knowing. He knew how to turn himself into a log or stump, for example, a talent you don't come across much anymore. He would sit down out in the woods, and in a few seconds he would blend into the earth with huckleberry brush sprouting out of his head and wild mushrooms poking out of his legs. Pretty soon, squirrels and chipmunks would be scampering around on him looking into his pockets and up his nostrils and wondering where this old rotting stump had suddenly come from. Many were the times I saw chipmunks race over the top of him, just like in a Walt Disney film, except the chipmunks in the film never gagged.

Speaking of gagging, I recall the first time I ever ate any of Rancid's homemade jerky. I was pedaling my bike past his cabin one day when he bellowed at me to stop.

"Ah want you to try this," he said, as I dismounted. He dug into a greasy paper bag and pulled out a black, twisted object that looked like a dried mole or maybe something one might find in the vicinity of a small camel. A tremor of dread flowed through my taste buds.

"What is it?" I asked, hoping it wasn't something intended for human consumption.

"Ain't you ever seen jerky before?"

"Nope."

"Wahl, this here is some b'ar jerky ah jist made. Ah made it the old way, smoked it over a willer fahr down by the crick."

He started to hand me the dried mole, then suddenly jerked it back and held the thing up close to his eyes. "Danged bugs!" he growled, snapping a speck off the mole with a grimy finger. "Looks like ah made jerky out of some of them too. Har!"

Failing to share Rancid's mirth over the fate of the bug, I sorted through my vast file of falsehoods in the hope of finding one that would demand my immediate departure. None came to mind. So I accepted the jerky, popping it into my mouth like, say, a piece of bear jerky dried and smoked over a willow fire. It lay like a time bomb on my tongue. I was afraid to disturb it.

"Wahl, whatcha thank?"

I smiled faintly. "Mmmm."

"Ah thank so too. Funny thang, though, ah cain't git the dog even to try it."

Presently it became apparent that the dog was a creature of uncommon good sense. The dried mole, responding to the moist environment of my mouth, began to take on a life of its own. It began to swell. I gave a brief wave, leaped on my bike, and headed for home, hoping to be out of the sight of Rancid before I spit out the mole. I was surprised it just lay there in the dirt and didn't race off into the brush. Many years later, when I was much older and knew better, I accepted from an old trapper another piece of bear jerky that had been smoked and dried over a willow fire. Bear jerky hadn't improved one bit in all those years.

Rancid prided himself on his knowledge of wild foods. One day when we were climbing the mountain back of his cabin, he suddenly stooped and ripped some leaves off a plant. "Ever eat miner's lettuce?" he asked, popping some in his mouth. He then made a terrible face and spit out the half-chewed leaves. "Wahl, this ain't it! You remember what ah'm telling you now. Don't never eat leaves thet look like these ones."

Along with other such bits of woodcraft and nature lore, Rancid taught me just about everything I needed to know about fear of the dark. He was pretty sure evil spirits haunted certain parts of the woods, and he made a point of avoiding such after dark. Among his vast knowledge of nature lore was the belief that owls could communicate with us humans. Most of the things they had to say weren't worth listening to, but if one said your name, you were in deep trouble. You were a goner. Even to this day, when an owl speaks, a shudder runs up my spine, just thinking about it. A friend of mine claims that when he was a little boy he heard an owl speak his name. He's in his sixties now, and I still don't want to break the bad news to him. Oddly, most of what I regard as Rancid's nonsense has somehow taken up residence in the back of my mind.

Among a thousand other things Rancid taught me was to always be prepared. On the opening day of trout season one spring, he had promised to take me fishing. I arrived at his cabin at precisely 4:30 in the morning. He had told me if I was a minute late, he was leaving without me. Surprised not to find him sitting on his porch, fishing pole in hand, I gently pushed open the cabin door. There he was, still in his bunk, snoring loudly.

"Wake up, Rancid!" I yelled. "You said you would be ready and waiting and you aren't even awake yet, let alone dressed!"

"Wha?" he said, his eyes popping open. "What you mean, ah ain't even dressed?" He threw off the covers and walked out the door, fully clothed, right down to his boots.

"You sleep with all your clothes on?" I said.

"Why not?" he said. "Otherwise, you just got to put 'em back on in the morning."

That's advice I've always remembered. Even after all these years, my wife still says, "I hate the opening day of trout season!"

When I got to be seventeen, I went out and got a job and didn't see much of Rancid after that, but I knew he was disappointed in me. Then I went to college and later went to work as a newspaper and television reporter. By then, I had a wife and four daughters and numerous pets and was tied down with other various kinds of employment. Suddenly, my writing took off and earned me a modest living, so I wasn't tied down with a job anymore. My wife and I could live anywhere. The girls had gone off to college. All this time, I had nurtured the hope of someday becoming just as independent as Rancid Crabtree, living out in the woods and off the land and free as a bird.

So one day—my wife and I were about forty, as I recall—we bought ourselves a piece of land on a river, built a cabin there, and planted a huge garden and fruit trees and nut trees and berry bushes, and I cut our firewood out of the national forest and shot game and picked wild berries and mushrooms and caught fish out of the river. It was just like I had dreamed. Crabtree knew how to live, all right, even if he didn't have electric lights and television and taxes to pay. Living free and wild takes a lot of work, though, and you get awfully tired. One winter, the snow on the island got so deep there wasn't any more room in which to plow it. That's when we moved back to town and bought ourselves a condo. Still, I have fond memories of living the fantasy, and friends of mine often say, "It sounds like a wonderful way to live. Will you ever go back to it?" I allow my face to take on a dreamlike expression, just for effect. Then I say, "Not in a million years!"

Christmas Shopping

M y wife, Bun, told me the other day that I didn't have to worry about my annual Christmas shopping venture to find her an appropriate gift. "Anyway, if I want something I'll simply go out and buy it," she said.

"Wonderful," I said. "But surely there's some little thing I could purchase for you, something to put under the tree."

"Well, yes, there is," she said. "Underwear."

"No!" I screamed. "Not underwear! I hate the way all the clerks look at me as if I'm some kind of pervert strolling about through the lingerie department."

Bun laughed. "You won't have to be embarrassed shopping for this gift. It's long underwear. The days are already turning cold, and I just think long underwear might be very nice, particularly when I'm out tidying up the yard on chilly days."

Hmm, ladies' long underwear, I thought. That doesn't sound at all like something a pervert would be pawing through piles of pink dainties to find.

"Furthermore," Bun went on, "ladies' long underwear usually comes in two pieces, but I don't need the top. I have lots of warm tops. Just buy the bottom."

Perfect! I thought. A gentleman would never buy long underwear for his mistress, so there is no worry there. Furthermore, he wouldn't buy only the bottoms. I could see no downside to buying the bottom piece of a pair of ladies' long underwear.

Then Bun said, "Also, I tend to get a rash on my legs from wool underwear. So try to find something soft and creamy. And white. Get white! I don't want something blazing red."

"Certainly not," I said. "White it is."

A few days later, I found myself peering out over the vast lingerie department of a huge department store. It seemed to take up nearly half the second floor. I skirted around the outside edge of the department. From the huge pillars hung full-size pictures of nearly-naked young women. Every few feet I would feign a yawn, casually glancing this way and that, as if searching for my spouse. Apparently, long underwear for women was not a big seller. At least, I didn't see any on display. I saw only one man slowly making his way through the department, occasionally reaching out and rubbing a bit of pink flimsy material between his thumb and forefinger— clearly a pervert. On the other hand, there were a number of gentlemen like myself, patrolling the outer edge of the lingerie department, occasionally glancing over its vastness as if in search of a wife.

I had expected to see a display of long underwear, at which point I would dart over, snatch up a pair of bottoms, and rush back to the checkout counter. It only stood to reason that somewhere in that vastness of pink, a display of women's long underwear would suddenly stand out like a beacon, but, alas, nothing. All I could do was find and ask the clerk at a checkout counter about the availability of such an item in the store or anywhere I might find such a thing.

The checkout lady was middle-aged with perfectly coiffed gray hair, and a pencil tucked behind her ear. She appeared to be the kind of no-nonsense salesperson I was hoping to find.

"Yes, may I help you, sir?" she said.

I cleared my throat and tried to look normal. "Do you by any chance have a white creamy bottom . . . ?" I began. She looked startled.

"Underwear!" I stammered. "A long underwear bottom. I'm looking for a pair of white long underwear but only the bottom part. For my wife. And she said she would like white and creamy, if I could find it."

"Yes, sir," the lady said, smiling. "I know exactly what you are looking for." She waded off through the sea of pink and soon returned carrying a tube, the size three tennis balls fit in. How could I have missed it? On the outside of the tube was an illustration of a long underwear bottom. I was relieved, having half-expected the clerk to return with a store detective. She seemed quite accustomed to customers of my type, however, and said, "No wonder you couldn't find it, sir. I don't know why they put long underwear in tubes anyway. It says here on the side that it's creamy and white."

I paid and thanked her, perhaps a bit too profusely, and scurried away with my tube of long underwear bottoms.

Next Christmas I'll just buy Bun a mink. I don't know where I can buy one that's house-broken, but it will be a lot easier than finding a lady's long underwear bottom.

Who Ate My Shakespeare?

Most of our family pets over the years were illiterate, but we had one gerbil with a love for Shakespeare. During his many escapes from his cage, he ate halfway through a volume of Shakespeare's plays. It did not improve him intellectually, as far as we could tell, but he clearly loved the old bard. Each time he got out, he sampled more of him.

During one of his escapes, he was on the lam for nearly a month. I don't know how he survived, and clearly he wouldn't have if I ever got my hands on him. My wife and I and our four young daughters lived in a ratty mobile home just off the campus of Washington State University, and I suspect one of the women folk smuggled bits of cheese and other goodies to the rodent. Not that he needed food. His last escape lasted for many weeks, during which time he gnawed away at most of my library, but seemed to favor Shakespeare over the lesser authors.

Wilson, the gerbil, was not our only pet rodent. Our menagerie also included hamsters and guinea pigs, as well as rabbits, two cats, and a dachshund, the latter going about with a worried look and complaining endlessly about his fellow pets.

The guinea pig was named Jack, after the president at the time, John F. Kennedy, because they had similar hairstyles, as I recall.

One morning I was sleeping late when I awakened to the cry, "Dad! Dad! Jack is loose!" I mulled this over in my mind. Was it bad news or good news? Then my wife rushed into the bedroom.

"Jack got out and is running down the alley! You've got to go catch him! Quick!"

Perhaps responding to the general panic, I leaped out of bed wearing only my boxer shorts, tore out of the house, and rushed to the alley. We were now living in the middle of a city with numerous police officers who regarded persons rushing about in their boxer shorts as real or potential criminals. I hurtled our back fence that had a hole through which the escapee had made his getaway.

Two houses down, I could see the miserable rodent ambling merrily on his way, pausing from time to time to take in the scenery or munch the blossom of a dandelion. Sensing that I was closing in on him, Jack suddenly darted under a backyard fence. I vaulted the fence and snatched him up. That was when I noticed an elderly lady lunging at me with her hand trowel, a frightened snarl growing on her face. She had been crouched down weeding her flower bed next to the fence and apparently was unaccustomed to strange men wearing only boxer shorts leaping into her yard. The strange man instantly leaped back over the fence and fled back down the alley, carrying the escaped rodent, which the elderly lady no doubt thought he was planning to eat.

I really have no excuse for my despicable action later that morning, other than that Jack's escape and the violent old lady had put me in a terrible mood.

My wife said, "Oh, you get dressed and have some coffee, and I'll fry you some shaggymanes for breakfast."

For many years, Bun and I collected the delicious wild mushrooms each fall, chopped them up, and froze them in little containers as a special treat for ourselves. Still grumpy, I sat at the breakfast table awaiting the arrival of my mushrooms. Here I must mention that I have a friend who is an excellent poet. Income for poets being what it is, he also worked at the time as a night watchman at a warehouse. The job often left him with time on his hands during the night shift. He used it to write poems. The poems were often dark and dreary, reflecting his mood in the lonely, late hours of the night. I'll call him Melvin. Mel had made a practice of showing up right after work each morning to read me his most recent poems. I would invite him to eat breakfast with me. He would say, "Oh, no. I don't want to eat your breakfast."

"Well, have a piece of toast anyway."

"OK a piece of toast. Pass the jam."

"Scrambled egg?"

"Oh, I guess. Are you done with the bacon?"

And so on. Nearly every morning we went through this ritual while Melvin read me his night's output.

The poems did not put me in a good mood. On this particular morning, I said, "Have some mushrooms, Mel."

"Wow, mushrooms for breakfast," he said. "Yeah, I'll have some."

I gave him a hefty serving. He sampled them tentatively and then dug in with gusto. "Man, these are really delicious. What kind are they?"

"I don't know," I said. "I found them growing out in the backyard."

His fork clattered against the empty plate. Without saying a word, he leaped to his feet and walked out the door. I didn't see him again for six weeks. I've always wondered if he rushed off to an emergency room to have his stomach pumped or what, but I've never felt the urge to mention mushrooms to him again. It is best to avoid eating breakfast with a man who has just rushed down an alley in his under shorts to save a guinea pig and been attacked by a crazy old lady with a gardening trowel. It brings out the worst in him.

Romantic Moments

My wife, Bun, and I were watching a dumb old film on TV the other night, one of those films in which the man and woman spend about half the movie running and laughing through the rain and not so much as a single shot is fired the whole time and not one car goes up in a ball of flames and at the end they get married in a hot-air balloon and float off together into the sunset.

"And they have the nerve to call this a movie!" I shouted as the names of the four thousand people it took to make this piece of fluff scrolled up our television screen.

Bun smiled through her tears. "I loved it! Oh, when he gave her that beautiful little music box, and then they went running and laughing through the rain—that was so romantic! I wish you were romantic."

"Me? I am romantic. Remember when I gave you that new toaster for your birthday? I remember thinking we could very easily take this toaster out and run and laugh through the rain."

Bun shook her head. "You are many things, some even socially acceptable, but you are not romantic!"

"No, really, I am. I just go to great pains to conceal it. Why, when I was ten years old I made quite a study of romance."

"Really? Maybe I should have known you when you were ten years old. So what was this romance you studied?"

"The romance of my sister, the Troll. I was ten and she was sixteen, the perfect situation for scientific research."

"I bet. Your sister had to put up with a little brat of a brother when she was sweet sixteen?"

"Just plain sixteen. I never detected any sweet. That's why I called her the Troll. For some reason that my scientific methodology failed to detect, boys were attracted to her. I remember one miserable specimen by the name of Derwood. He drove a blue coupe with a rumble seat. Whenever they went for a drive, my mother would make me go along in the rumble seat. Both the the Troll and Derwood hated me. I sometimes thought about Derwood's car going up in a ball of flames. It emitted so much exhaust that I thought it was about to go at any minute, but it never did. Sometimes they would sit out in the swing on the front porch and talk and giggle. I never once saw them run through the rain, but they may have. Derwood was about that dumb. Anyway, one day they were sitting in the swing, and my friend Crazy Eddie Muldoon and I were lying in one of my mother's flower beds next to the porch doing scientific research on them and . . . "

"Snooping, we used to call that," Bun said. "I'm just so glad I didn't have a little brother when you and I were dating."

"Yeah," I said. "I would have had to tie him in a gunnysack and drop him in the river."

"Nonsense. We never did anything out of line."

"Oh, that must have been some other girl."

Bun gave me a murderous look.

"Oh, I just remembered. There weren't any other girls. You were my first and only girlfriend. Now, isn't that romantic?"

"I suppose," she said. "On the other hand, I just thought of something even more romantic."

"Really?"

"Yes," she said. "I have to go fix supper, and you can peel the potatoes."

"I'd rather run laughing through the rain," I said.

Mother's Day is coming up, and I usually buy Bun a gift, even though technically I don't think the husbands of mothers are required to do so. We have four daughters and umpteen grandchildren, and they usually come through with a ton of gifts. Still, my romantic side feels compelled to buy Bun something romantic. I've been thinking of a potato peeler. Not just one of those hand-operated ones, but something you drop the potato in and it buzzes off the skin. Otherwise a lot of hand labor goes into to peeling spuds.

Bun likes to clean. I've never been into cleaning much myself, but she seems to like it. Personally, I tend to think of semi-mess as clean. The problem is that Bun has a whole closet full of brooms and mops and vacuums and even some little whiffler things for getting dust out from under davenports and other stuff where the dust can't be seen anyway. Hey, if it can't be seen, why bother?

She says, "I think the same about you, but even when just the two of us are home, you tend to be a bit of a mobile mess. A lovable mobile mess, but still a mess."

"I clean up pretty good, though," I counter.

"Yes, I remember."

As a matter of fact, I'd better get cleaned up, if I'm going out to buy Bun a Mother's Day present. The boys at the hardware store don't mind one way or the other, but Bun likes me to be presentable any time I leave the house. You'd think I was going to a royal wedding rather than to a hardware store, but that's just the way she is.

Hey, it's starting to rain. I wonder if Bun would . . . naw, I'll wait until Mother's Day.

The Canoe

When Retch Sweeney and I drove up in Mrs. Peabody, our mountain car, Retch's father was sitting on the front porch having himself a beer and a cigar. Mrs. Peabody never liked to be turned off so when Retch flipped the ignition switch, she continued to roar, bellow, smoke, and steam, finally giving up only after emitting an explosive backfire that raised Mr. Sweeney a good six inches off the porch. Mrs. Peabody, named in honor of our favorite high school English teacher, had provided us with many good laughs, and this was one of them.

Disheveled and covered with beer foam and cigar ashes, Mr. Sweeney glared at us as we came up the walk.

"Gave you a little start, huh, Popper?" Retch said, still chuckling.

"One of these days . . . " Mr. Sweeney said. It was his favorite expression.

Retch pointed to five steel barrels lashed to the roof of Mrs. Peabody. "What do you think of our canoe?"

"Canoe?" Mr. Sweeney said, staring at the barrels.

"Yep. Of course, they ain't a canoe yet. See, what Pat and me are gonna do is cut the tops and bottoms out of the barrels. Then we'll split them down the center, spread them open, and weld them together in a straight line. What do you think, Popper?"

"I think it will sink like a rock," Mr. Sweeney growled.

"Don't joke, Popper. This is serious. Now where's your welding outfit?"

There then ensued one of those loud, nasty family arguments that a visitor finds so embarrassing. Mrs. Sweeney came out on the porch to intervene and just in the nick of time, too, for I was of the clear impression that Mr. Sweeney was trying to get his hands around Retch's throat.

"Shush, you two," Mrs. Sweeney said. "What will the neighbors think?"

Mr. Sweeney released his son, and Retch squawked, "We just want to use Popper's welder for a little bit."

Mrs. Sweeney frowned at Popper. "Don't be such a grouch, Harold. Let the boys use your welder. It's good for youngsters to work with their hands. Keeps them out of trouble."

Retch said, "Yeah, Popper, Pat, and me built Mrs. Peabody ourselves, didn't we?"

"My point exactly," Mr. Sweeney said.

The truth was that Mr. Sweeney had used up several days of his vacation assembling confusing piles of wreckage scattered about the floor of his garage into what was now Mrs. Peabody. This may have explained why he responded to Retch's utterance with a maniacal laugh, a sound which never failed to stir the short hairs on the back of my neck.

Mr. Sweeney finally gave in, and said we could use his welding outfit. "Just don't burn down the garage, that's all I ask."

It seemed little enough to ask.

The cutting and welding of the barrels went along smoothly, at least until Retch put the torch to the last barrel. Mr. Sweeney was on his back porch now, glumly sprinkling the lawn with a garden hose. Retch stepped to the garage door and asked, "Popper, where do we keep the fire extinguisher?"

"There's one in the truck," Mr. Sweeney said. "Put it back when . . . FIRE EXTINGUISHER!"

He bounded off the porch and out to his truck, snatched up the fire extinguisher, and managed to extinguish the fire before it reached his workbench.

Retch said, "I guess there was a little oil or something in that last barrel."

"Unnnhhhh!" Mr. Sweeney said, twitching.

Mrs. Sweeney had rushed out to see what all the commotion was about. "Good heavens, Harold!" she cried. "Be more careful. You could have burned down the garage!"

"Unnnhhhh!" Mr. Sweeney replied.

"Say, Popper," Retch said. "Since you ain't doing nothing, why don't you help us shape the bow of the canoe?"

"That's a wonderful idea!" Mrs. Sweeney said. "I think it's so nice when you help the boys with their little projects."

Mr. Sweeney muttered something.

"Harold! How many times do I have tell you—don't use that word!"

Mr. Sweeney finally shaped the last barrel into a very faint resemblance of a canoe bow, while Retch and I were sawing off lengths of angle iron to use as thwarts. Shortly thereafter, the canoe was finished. You would never guess it had been made out of five steel barrels. The gunnels were a bit wavy, but that certainly wouldn't affect the performance of the canoe. Now all that remained was for Retch and me to carry the canoe out of the garage and hoist it onto the top of Mrs. Peabody. But by straining to the maximum, we moved it only a foot or so. Mr. Sweeney stood there, hands on his hips, watching us. Then in one fluid motion he grabbed the canoe, hauled it out of his garage, and threw it atop Mrs. Peabody. "Now get it out of my sight!" he yelled.

Retch and I stepped back to admire our canoe. "Look at that baby!" Retch said. "I bet it will last a hundred years!"

"Two hundred years!" I said.

"Three seconds," Popper said.

Each barrel used in the canoe was a different color—red, blue, green, and rust. The seams welded with coat-hanger wire as a substitute for welding rod and bordered with burnt paint gave it a primitive look, assuming primitive canoe builders had access to welders and metal barrels and possessed minimum talent.

Mrs. Sweeney came out to admire our accomplishment. "Oh, it looks wonderful! Be sure to wear life preservers when you test it. Now, Harold, I want you to go out with the boys and keep an eye on them to make sure they don't get hurt or drown if their boat tips over. You know how boys are."

"Know how boys are!" Mr. Sweeney said in a voice very much like a horse's whinny.

"Don't worry about us, Ma," Retch said. "We're taking along a truck inner tube as a life preserver. Oh, yeah, I almost forgot. We need to get the oars out of Popper's boat to use as paddles."

"Not on your life!" shouted Mr. Sweeney. "You're not touching my oars!"

"Harold!"

Half an hour later, we were headed out to Sand Creek for a test run. Now at flood stage, Sand Creek had overflowed its banks and formed a small, calm lake out in the middle of a pasture, a perfect launching place for the canoe. The creek, however, was an ugly brown current churning along and eating away at its banks, carrying off trees, fence posts, and various other spoils.

Contrary to Mr. Sweeney's predictions, the barrel canoe floated like a cork, although a somewhat tippy cork. Retch and I got in, Mr. Sweeney shoved us off with his foot, and we paddled happily around on the little lake.

"What do you think, Popper?" Retch called out.

"Looks good. Better than I expected. I think it will hold all three of us."

"What did I tell you?" Retch said to me.

Mr. Sweeney arranged the inner tube in the middle of the canoe and sat his rear end down in the middle of it.

"All right, me hearties!" he shouted. "Cast off!"

We paddled about the little lake for twenty minutes or so, getting the feel of the canoe. It floated wonderfully well. Even Mr. Sweeney said so. The only problem was the tipping, but as Mr. Sweeney pointed out, the secret was to pretend you were riding a bike. You had to keep your balance.

Retch soon tired of the placid water. "Let's take her down the crick a ways!" he shouted. "Hold on, Popper!"

Even as Mr. Sweeney croaked out, "Wait! Stop!" Retch thrust the canoe into the brown, swirling current of Sand Creek.

To Mr. Sweeney's surprise, as he said later, the craft appeared exceedingly creek-worthy, and the three of us relaxed and enjoyed the pleasant float. "Hold her steady, boys," he said. "Hold her steady." He dug out a cigar, lit it, and relaxed in his inner tube, enjoying a smoke.

As we rounded a bend, I was the first to spot trouble ahead. The foundation of a railroad bridge sent a large, nasty, diagonal wave across the creek. I could see that the canoe would not survive the wave. At the bow end as the canoe passed the abutment, I stood up and stepped off on to it. Retch, paddling in the stern, did the same when his end of the canoe came by. The canoe instantly vanished beneath the waves.

Although the loss of the canoe pained Retch and me a great deal, Mr. Sweeney lucked out. He got his picture in the newspaper. A photographer snapped a photo of him floating in an inner tube down the flood-swollen creek, a cigar clenched in his mouth. He was rescued by sheriff's deputies, and Mr. Sweeney was even luckier to have the photographer record that. It made Popper famous throughout the whole county, and for years afterward his feat was remembered by most of the county.

"Geez, Popper," Retch said to him. "You're a local celebrity!"

As Retch admitted later, it was apparently the wrong thing to say.

The Writing of "The Green Box"

I have written humor columns for New York magazines for nearly fifty years. A casual observer of the craft might assume we humor writers simply skim comic ideas off the tops of our heads. Not so. Much care and deliberation go into the creation of the idea for each humor piece. Here is an example of the complexities of the humor-writing process.

Many years ago, New York editors figured out that by taking advantage of the three-hour time difference between New York and Spokane, Washington, where I live, they could phone and catch me asleep and unaware at five o'clock in the morning. I, therefore, wouldn't have any time to think up any lies about why I had missed a deadline or some other inconsequential thing.

So one morning at about five, or maybe it was seven or eight, I was suddenly awakened by the ringing of the phone next to my bed. Still groggy from sleep, I answered it.

Without so much as a "hello," a gruff voice growled in my ear: "It had better be in the mail!"

At the time, I was writing a monthly column for an outdoor magazine, and, consequently, had no trouble guessing the identity of the caller. It was editor Dave Psinsky, as I'll call him here, the managing editor of the magazine.

I instantly realized Dave was calling about my column. I wasn't too surprised he hadn't received it yet. I hadn't mailed it yet. I hadn't written it yet. I hadn't even thought about writing it. The only decent thing to do was for me to confess my error and plead for mercy. So I said, "What! You haven't received it yet?"

"You mailed it?" Dave said. "The [bleeping] post office! Well, maybe it will arrive today."

"You never can tell," I said.

I figured I was off the hook for the moment. I'd get busy right away, think up an idea for the piece, write it, mail it, and blame the whole delay on the post office.

Then Dave said, "Wait a minute. I need to get the artist started on the illustration right away. Describe one of the big scenes to me."

"Hmm," I said. "There are so many big scenes."

By then I had been writing magazine pieces for a long time, and I knew it was a good idea to have a little conflict in each story. So I said, "My wife and I are having an argument."

"OK got it," Dave said. "Are you having this argument in the kitchen or where?"

"Outside," I said. "By the garage."

"What are you arguing about?"

"A big box," I said.

"OK," Dave said. "What's the outdoor angle?"

"The outdoor angle? Well, the box is full of a bunch of outdoor stuff—old fishing rods, and like that."

"So what's the argument about?"

"Uh, Bun wants me to throw the old stuff away."

"OK This box any particular color?"

"Green," I said.

"What's the title of the piece?"

"The Green Box."

So there is an example of all the thought and stress that goes into writing for a New York outdoor magazine. Do you have any idea how hard it is to write a 2,500-word piece about a stupid green box?

A Routine Fishing Trip

For twenty years we had a place on the Clark Fork River near the town of Clark Fork, Idaho. Nothing seemed to go right there. There were always problems. It was one of the few places in the world where I felt at home.

One day I got a call from a Portland, Oregon, TV producer who told me he was bringing a crew up to do a feature on me. I told him my friend Dave Lisaius and I would meet him and his crew in Spokane, and they could follow us up to our fishing spot on the Clark Fork River. The producer said that sounded great, just the sort of angle he was looking for.

So Dave and I met the producer and his crew in Spokane and started off toward the Clark Fork River, about eighty miles away. I was driving my old pickup truck, my canoe strapped to a carrier on top. As we were passing a tire company near a small Idaho town, we heard the distinct thumping of a flat tire—this sound was familiar to both Dave and me and not the sort of thing that caused us any concern. Alas, it turned out my spare tire was also flat. This came as something of a surprise to me, because usually *two* of my tires go flat when I am far back in the mountains. In this case, I had pulled right into the parking lot of a national tire company. I explained to the TV crew that this sort of thing usually didn't happen to me. They apparently assumed I meant getting two flat tires at once, rather than being lucky enough for the flats to occur right next to a tire company. I explained to the crew that I would simply buy a couple of new tires, have one of them installed by the tire company, and we would be on our way. The producer didn't respond well to this news, apparently because he had something called a "deadline" that evening. I had heard of deadlines before but had always found them easy to ignore. Apparently television was a whole different medium. It made me nervous. I ran into the tire company and told them what I needed. The manager sauntered out of his office and said it would be two hours before his people could get to me. I went out and told the producer. He started jumping up and down. I suggested they start shooting our fishing trip right there, even though there wasn't any water in sight. He smiled. "OK, we might as well." Soon they had all the TV cameras out and were about to start taping me trying to change the flat with the tire company in the immediate background. At that point, the manager came running out and said he'd suddenly had a cancellation and could take care of my tires right then. Soon we were on the road again.

Presently, we arrived at our fishing spot. It wasn't the fishing spot I had planned on but a different one, because I had gotten distracted over all the problems with tires. Finally, we got the canoe launched on this unknown section of the Clark Fork River. It was then that I discovered we had forgotten the paddles. I say "we" because Dave is supposed to remind me of the paddles, because I almost always forget them. He has one responsibility, and he forgets it. I told the producer that this wasn't a serious problem, because Dave and I often used pieces of driftwood for paddles. The producer jumped up and down and pulled at his hair, while the crew got out the cameras and started shooting footage of Dave and me paddling around with two pieces of driftwood. After a while we caught a fish. It was about seven inches long. An hour or so later, we caught another fish but it was small. So far the fishing trip had been pretty much routine for Dave and me, but I could tell the producer hadn't had much experience with the art of angling. Dave and I regard fishing as a relaxing activity, but it was clear the producer wasn't enjoying himself nearly as much as we and his crew were.

Several weeks later, the TV station sent me copies of the feature, and it was wonderful, particularly in its realistic capture of fishing as a sport. After the first segment, the announcer on the show said to its producer, "I understand, John, this is the first time you've ever gone fishing." The producer said, "Yes, Fred, it is. But never again!"

So, it was just as I had suspected.

The Brown Pelican

I was just sitting here on the sixth-floor balcony of a resort hotel (*borrr-ing!*) in Florida, three thousand miles from my home in the Pacific Northwest, when a brown pelican flew by. It's the first time I have seen a brown pelican. For that matter, it's the first time a brown pelican has ever seen me. I seem to be the only one of the two of us who was impressed. The pelican, by all appearances, couldn't have cared less.

I have been doing a lot of reading about brown pelicans lately. Well, not really. Any reading at all about brown pelicans probably seems like a lot. There isn't that much written about brown pelicans, or any other color of pelicans, for that matter. Nevertheless, I have been reading a hotel pamphlet about them. To me, they are much more interesting than, say, Wall Street raiders, Donald Thump, Porter Sims, or Zsa Zsa McShane, who right now are all the rage with the news magazines and newspapers. On the other hand, you could probably read all the publications on a supermarket magazine rack for a year and not come across a single word about brown pelicans.

One of the interesting things I've learned about pelicans—the brown ones, at least—is that when they dive into the water, they turn over on their backs a split second before impact. Supposedly, they do this to keep from breaking their necks. I wonder how pelicans discovered this. I can imagine a long history of pelicans in neck braces, before one of them accidentally flipped over on his back before striking the water—"Hey, guys, I think I've got it!"

My literature on brown pelicans reveals that they strike the water with such force that the target fish is stunned, and then the pelican gobbles it up. There seems to be some similarity here with the way Wall Street raiders strike their victims—a different kind of fish, of course. Perhaps the raiders have studied the pelican's fishing techniques. It would be interesting to know if they flip over on their backs just before the hit. I don't know that much about Wall Street raiders.

I regret to report that the brown pelican, unlike the Wall Street raider, is a threatened species. This may strike you as sad and even tragic, as it does me. I withheld the news from the brown pelican that just flew by, because I didn't want to ruin his day. I don't think there's anything he could do about his being threatened anyway. I suspect he's pretty ignorant about the whole business of extinction. Maybe one of the brown pelican's children asked him, "Daddy, what does 'extinct' mean?" And he tells the kid, "Don't bother me with your stupid questions, Jason. Go catch a fish! And remember to turn over on your back!"

The brown pelican appears to me to be another innocent bystander who's about to become a victim to the great environmental disaster known as the Twentieth Century. Every year, dozens, perhaps hundreds or thousands, of species become extinct. I'm sure no one knows exactly how many—or when. There might be a few tough old individuals of a species hiding out in a swamp or on a mountain somewhere, awaiting their chance to stage a comeback. Or maybe they don't even know their kind is about to be extinct. They might just wonder why none of their friends or relatives visit any more. He thinks, "Maybe I have bad breath. Maybe it's my unsightly dandruff." You wouldn't want to tell him, "No, you idiot, your species is going extinct!"

It's hard to get worked up about the extinction of a species you never knew existed in the first place. Species come and species go, you say. The problem is that, during my lifetime, a few thousand species have gone, and I haven't heard of a single one coming back. We're running a deficit on species. We have a species-flow problem. Of course, maybe some species have come online that I haven't heard about. I don't get around all that much, and people don't make a habit of calling me to report new species. Maybe where you live, new species are popping up all over the place. I hope that's the case. I also hope none of these new species are flying snakes or that sort of thing. Flying cows would be bad, too. ("We interrupt this broadcast to report a low-flying-cow alert for the Denver area. Stay tuned for further details.")

Extinction, in my opinion, is not totally bad, as long as it's happening to the other guy, of course. I doubt if people would get too worked up to read the following news story: "Tragedy struck Thursday in Two Dot, Montana, when Molly, the world's last surviving mosquito, escaped from her cage and landed on the neck of a passing cowboy, who. . . ."

And how about pterodactyls, those vicious giant flying reptiles that lived back in dinosaur days, one of the least popular times for picnics? Suppose pterodactyls didn't become extinct. Suppose right now you're sitting in your duck blind and a flock of pterodactyls come flapping in over your decoys. ("Hush, Sport, hush!") You see what I mean? Extinction isn't all bad.

Speaking of pterodactyls, does anyone know for sure what happened to them? Did they just suddenly die off, to the resounding cheers of the other creatures then extant, or did they slowly blend into another species, such as our own? Impossible, you say, but then you probably never saw my Uncle Shamus. Talk about your weird coincidences—my Uncle Shamus is also extinct now. So how do you figure that? As my mother used to be fond of saying, it just goes to show.

I hope the preceding thoughts and reflections give you some idea of just how boring it is to be sitting here on a tiny sixth-floor balcony in a Florida resort hotel. The only thing of interest to happen in the last hour was that a plump lady walked by the pool in a bikini so tight she looked as if she was about to be shot out of it. Oh, yes, and a brown pelican flew by. Well, the brown pelican hasn't come by again. I hope he hasn't gone and done something stupid, like become extinct. You know how it is, forget just one time to flip over on your back when you dive for a fish and, *whop*, you're history.

Canoodled

All my life, I have loved canoes. I like anything that floats: inner tubes, float tubes, my boat-in-a-bag, rubber rafts, kayaks, rowboats, yachts, and even ships, although nothing larger than a light cruiser. (Battleships and aircraft carriers are too hard to turn.) But it's only canoes I love. Otherwise, I'm fairly normal.

Kayaks are fine, except I have trouble putting them on and taking them off. Yachts are great, too, but if the motor won't start and you become the sole source of power, they're awfully hard to row. Also, they're difficult to store in your garage. You can shove a canoe up into the rafters, but let's see you try that with a yacht. There's an old saying, "If you can afford a yacht, you can afford to moor it." (Actually, the saying isn't that old. I made it up just five seconds ago).

One of the great hardships of my life is that I have never owned a jetboat. It's a terrible thing to admit, but there you go. Sometimes you simply become too distracted by work and other absurdities to focus on the important things in life.

If reincarnation exists, I will definitely buy a jetboat my next time around, even if it means observers might shout out, "Look! A squirrel driving a jetboat." There are certain risks to consider in regard to both jetboats and reincarnation.

I once wrote a book titled *They Shoot Canoes, Don't They?* For nearly forty years, canoe enthusiasts have bought that book like crazy. They actually think the book is about canoes! Ha! I haven't gone back and read the book in about forty years, so I'm not sure what it's about. It may even contain the story about how I came to marry my wife. Then again, maybe not.

I must confess that when I was young I was very particular about the women I dated. They had to be smart, beautiful, unmarried, and employed. A girl with the nickname of Bun had all those qualifications, and so one day I took her out for the final test—a canoe cruise down the North Fork of the Clearwater River in Idaho. At one point, the canoe swamped in rapids and Bun floated away in her life jacket, occasionally popping up through the whitewater on top of a towering wave. It was then that I noticed she was gathering up various flotsam of gear that had recently been in the bottom of the canoe. Although I don't regard it as an essential, I do appreciate tidiness in a spouse. At that very moment, I said, "Bun's the woman for me!"

On our honeymoon, I took Bun on a river float trip in the rain. As she confessed later, it was then she had her first doubts about the institution of marriage. Rafting or canoeing rivers is a wonderful test for a spouse. Bun says so herself.

But enough about romance.

At one point in my life, I owned three canoes. Being poor, I could not afford more. We lived next to a river at the time, so it was necessary to have a minimum of three canoes. One of the three was a thirteen-footer made of Kevlar. The ad for it claimed it could be dropped off the top of a ten-story building and survive unharmed. If you are not familiar with canoeing, you may not realize how often on a river you come upon something resembling a ten-story building; the sighting is usually announced by the lead canoeist shouting, "Holy bleep!" or a similar expression. That is a technical term often employed in canoeing.

Once a couple of my daughters took the thirteen-footer upriver and a wind storm arose, so they pulled the canoe up on a bank, tied it down, and walked home. If they are not particularly thoughtful of their father, they are at least sensible. Because it is quite easy for the wind to blow an empty canoe into the next state, I went up to get it and was soon paddling back home. When you paddle a thirteen-foot canoe alone, however, the whole front half tends to rise out of the water. This is especially bad in a strong wind. Despite my best efforts, the canoe soon began spinning like a top. I drifted downriver in this undignified fashion, the canoe totally out of control. As I spun past my house, I noticed Bun standing on the dock, hair blowing, hands on hips. She shouted, "Are you crazy! Stop fooling around out there and paddle in here!"

So you can see canoes aren't foolproof when it comes to selecting a spouse.

Another of my canoes was an eighteen-foot Old Town wood-and-canvas job. It was ancient but still gorgeous. Its one problem was that the previous owner had covered the canvas with fiberglass. This atrocity became apparent when you had to snap the canoe up the last quarter inch or so onto a cartop carrier all by yourself. If you weren't careful, you could easily hook the canoe on your eyeballs. Besides, the neighbors started complaining that my groans and grunts were scaring their pets. The time had come to sell the canoe, and I eventually found a young man appropriately appreciative of this superb craft. I helped him load it on his cartop carrier. As I watched the canoe disappearing down my driveway, I gave it a sad little wave. Then I shouted to the young man one last little canoeing tip: "Watch out for your eyeballs!"

I am now reduced to a single canoe, a seventeen-foot thin-skinned aluminum Grumman. It's a bit battered but otherwise in excellent shape, and I can pop it onto the cartop carrier with ease. The two of us, the canoe and I, have shared many an excellent adventure. Once on a hunting trip, my friend Retch Sweeney and I paddled it across a major Idaho lake during a late-November blizzard. The whole canoe was covered with frost—or maybe it was ice, I'm not sure now. As the bow paddler, I kept hearing this weird clicking sound, not especially unusual in a car but strange in a canoe. It turned out to be the chattering of Retch's teeth. Not all of our canoe outings were so much fun, though.

I first fell in love with canoes at about age ten. I was fishing along the creek that ran through the back of our farm when I suddenly came upon a canoe tied up to some brush in such a way that one might suppose its owner had attempted to hide it. Right away I guessed that it must belong to a teen-aged ruffian by the name of Buster. Despite his frequent threats to eradicate me from his life, I realized that Buster must be attempting amends, by leaving such a fine canoe tied up on my side of the creek.

Even after all these years, I possess a vivid image of that canoe. Clearly, Buster had built it himself, probably in no more than a thousand hours in high school shop class. The delicate wooden framework was covered in canvas, which the young builder had painted blue, apparently with house paint. Nevertheless, you could see the skeleton of the craft right through its taut skin. It was lovely.

Buster had been thoughtful enough even to the extent that he had left a paddle for me to use. Glancing about to make sure there were no immediate threats to my life—bears occasionally passed through our area—I slid down the bank and into the canoe. I quickly cleared away the brush that covered it, wondering all the while why Buster would be so careless with his property. I soon found the canoe much easier to paddle downstream than upstream, I don't know why. After a test float of a few hundred yards, and finding it extremely difficult to paddle back to the craft's original berth, I steered over to the bank and parked. Being a particularly thoughtful boy, I tied up the canoe in a place where Buster would have no trouble finding it. Then I went off home.

Later I thought maybe I should have wiped the canoe clean of my fingerprints, just in case Buster might be upset by someone's borrowing it. I was right, too. My fingerprints gave me away, no doubt about it, because Buster immediately zeroed in on me as his number one suspect. Boy, what I wouldn't have given for a witness protection program back in those days, the days I first fell in love with canoes.

Christmas Over Easy

One day my rich friend Fenton Quagmire said to me, "I'm sick of all this electronic gadgetry that kids want for Christmas nowadays. I wish we could go back to times when Christmas was simple, when kids made tree decorations by stringing popcorn and cranberries and making chains out of strips of colored paper."

I said, "I was a child in simple times and I remember that our Christmases were . . ."

"Stop!" cried Quagmire. "I never again want to hear about your simple times!"

But I would not be deterred, even though Quagmire pretended to cover his ears with his hands. He probably would have jumped up and left if I hadn't been driving him down the freeway at seventy miles an hour.

Back then, as I told Quagmire, my family lived far back in the mountains and we survived mostly on deer my father shot and fish he caught. There were no hunting and fishing seasons to abide by back then. There were game wardens, of course, but they lived in town and never came out of their houses unless disguised as real estate agents.

I went to first grade in our leaky old log cabin heated only by a barrel stove. The teacher, my Mom, chopped the firewood and dipped our drinking water out of a creek with a bucket. One day, a glowing coal shot out of a hole burned in the side of the barrel stove and set fire to the floor. Mom bounded across the room and stomped out the fire. Later she said she wished she had been wearing shoes. Teachers received very little pay in those simple days when hardly anyone bothered to pay taxes and people were happy.

"Stop!" cried Quagmire. "I can't breathe!"

As Christmas vacation approached, Mom put on a Christmas pageant for all the parents and neighbors. We kids sang carols and performed in a Christmas play Mom had written in her spare time. All the mothers enjoyed the pageant while the fathers gathered outside the school and passed around a bottle of something they referred to as "Christmas cheer."

Suddenly, Santa Claus himself, all dressed in red and adorned with his flowing white beard, bounded through the door and roared out, "Ho ho ho!" I almost had a heart attack. I'd always thought of Santa Claus as a figment of my father's imagination. But here was Santa in person! He went around the room and asked each pupil what he or she wanted for Christmas. He also gave each of us a candy cane slightly bigger than a newspaper question mark. When he bent over me to hear my request for a present, I was still shaken up by his abrupt appearance and couldn't think of anything I wanted. Then he was gone! But I did get one surprise—Santa drank whiskey! I could smell it on his breath!

A short while later, my mother said to my father, "I think we should spend Christmas at the farm." Yes, we did own a small farm, and because life was simple in those days we grew much of our own food. My father understood that when my mother used the phrase "I think," it was actually an order, as when she said to me, "I think you should go bring in some firewood."

Dad immediately went into action. He got a long stick and began probing the mounds of snow outside our cabin to see if he could detect our car. Once the vehicle was found, he dug it out and set about getting it started. Now you would think that an old car that had sat unused for months, one of them under a pile of snow, would be impossible to start. At the very least, its battery would be dead, there would be no way to charge it, and you couldn't call AAA for help, because there was no phone and probably no AAA anyway.

Aha! But because these were simple times, the car didn't depend on a battery to start. It had a crank! The crank was a crooked steel bar of sorts. You stuck one end of it in a hole in the front of the car and gave a quick turn to the other end. Sometimes the crank performed what was referred to as a "kickback," which, in an extreme case, whipped the cranker around and slapped him against the ground. But that was only in extreme cases. Usually it just dislocated a shoulder. Before he even started to crank, however, the cranker had to adjust the spark arrestor, which was operated by a little lever on the steering column. I'm not sure how it arrested the spark, but I think if you didn't have it set properly, you blew up your car.

Our car also had a rusty wire protruding from the dashboard. There was a loop in the wire that you could stick a finger through so you could pull or push it. I believe my father put the loop in the wire himself. He was always devising such innovations. He probably even devised the wire, now that I think about it. The other end of the wire, I believe, attached to either the throttle or choke on the engine or possibly both. The wire had to be set just right or the engine wouldn't start.

Now all of these functions required certain incantations to be shouted out by my father if success were to be achieved. I wish I could remember the words, because I think they would come in handy in the operation of this computer.

Before the car would move through the snow, however, my father had to attach to each rear wheel something called "chains." These were made out of steel links, some of which always came loose and banged against the inside of the fender, producing a sound very much like the firing of a machine gun as the car went down the road. Some war veterans dived into a ditch when our car went by. Nowadays, in these more complicated times, we have snow tires, some of which even have studs in them. People no longer bother with chains.

Once the car was started and chained up, we all piled in and headed off to the farm, which was about sixty miles distant. When we had traveled no more than three or four miles, we heard a peculiar thumping sound. My mother said to my father, "You have a flat, Frank. I think you should stop and fix it." My mother never said, "*We* have a flat." My father owned all the flats. Then my mother said, "I don't think you should use that kind of language in front of the children."

Darn! I wish I could remember some of the words!

Now you might suppose my father would get out and put on the spare. Ha! These were simple times, remember. There was no spare. Only rich people had spares. Actually, we didn't know any rich people, so I'm not sure whether they did or not. As for ourselves, we didn't have a spare anything. Everything we owned was in constant use.

Dad then got out, jacked up the car, took off the tire, jerked out the inner tube, patched the tube with a little patch kit everyone except rich people carried in their cars, stuffed the tube back in the tire, pumped up the tire with the tire pump, put the tire back on the car, lowered the jack, and we drove away. In these more complicated times, of course, even poor people have spares.

Quagmire found that disgusting. "Poor people shouldn't have spares!" he shouted. "What's the point of having poor people if they have everything rich people have?"

Settled in at the farm, my mother said to my father, "I think you should go cut us a Christmas tree." Dad rose up from the chair in which he had slumped and shouted out another incantation, this one somehow connected to the cutting of Christmas trees. He stormed out of the house and a few hours later returned with what he referred to as a Christmas tree. He then built a stand for it, which allowed the "tree" to stand, if you leaned it against a wall.

Mom said, "I think it looks more like a Christmas bush than a Christmas tree."

My sister and I made decorations for the Christmas bush. After Christmas, we ate the strings of popcorn and cranberries. Cranberries don't taste all that good after hanging on a Christmas bush for a week or so, but they're a lot better than nothing.

So that is an example of the simple-life Christmas, as I told Quagmire.

"Sounds pretty boring," he said, as I dropped him off at his mansion. "Come on in and have some Christmas cheer."

"I would," I said, "but right now I have to go Twitter."

Dog People

I've never been much of a dog person. That doesn't mean I don't like dogs. I do. I like them a lot. But mostly I like them if they belong to someone else. Dogs, in my opinion, should be much like grandchildren. Most of the time they're a lot of fun to have around, to play with, teach tricks to, throw sticks to, and so on. When they start acting up or otherwise making a nuisance of themselves, you should be able to send them home. Your dog, on the other hand, is already home. He isn't going anywhere.

My children all grew up with our family dogs, cats, horse, chickens, rabbits, gerbils, guinea pigs, and even a hamster that once escaped from his cage and, while on the lam for several weeks, ate its way through a volume of Shakespeare's plays, although with little sign of intellectual improvement. All of these creatures created endless problems for me, the horse taking first prize in the competition for great nuisance but the dogs running a close second. I had an excuse for buying the horse, though. I was insane. In fact, I had a professional opinion to that effect.

"I just bought a horse," I told my friend, who happens to be a clinical psychologist.

"You gotta be crazy!" he said.

When buying or otherwise acquiring dogs, I was always of sound mind. My only defense in that regard is stupidity, for which there would be no shortage of witnesses, professional or otherwise.

My problem is I'm a fool for puppies. Actually, I'm a fool for cute. I like cute puppies, kittens, children, and women. You can have all the beautiful women you want, I'll take the cute ones. *Whoa!* What am I saying? I can't take any women because I'm already married to one. She's very cute, though.

Either God or nature has made puppies cute for a purpose, namely to get innocent people to adopt the cuddly little things in the belief they will remain that way forever. A year after you acquire the cute puppy, a hulking brute lumbers into your kitchen, a piece of your new waders dangling from his mouth, and demands, "Give me meat or else. I know where you keep the split-bamboo fly rods."

Anytime someone holds up a cute little puppy for you to see, try to visualize it as a hulking brute, picking its teeth with some splinters from split-bamboo fly rods.

There was a time in my early youth when I spent many a great free golden summer running with dogs, going to the dogs, inseparable from the dogs, and, as my mother sometimes pointed out, being almost indistinguishable from the dogs. Some of the dogs were our own unruly mutts, others were those of neighbors, and some were simply strangers that had been passing through but got caught up in the fun and, no doubt, a chance at a free meal. I was Warrior King of Dogs and led my pack of canines off on great crusades across the creek, through the woods, and into the mountains. "Don't worry," my grandmother would tell my mother. "The dogs will show him the way home."

"I'm not worried," Mom would reply.

Once one of the dogs passing through didn't pass all the way through. He spent several days ingratiating him with my grandmother, mother, and sister. My sister said to my mother, "I know he's ugly as sin, but he's such a friendly little guy I think we should keep him."

"Of course we'll keep him," Mom replied. "He's your brother."

As it happened, we were short a dog at the time. My mother, a keen judge of both people and dogs, was reluctant. "Well," she said, "I guess he can stay for a while," she said, possibly because she didn't know how to get rid of him anyway. Mom named the dog Stranger. Mom said that way when we spoke to the dog while company was present, they would think we didn't own him. "Hey there, Stranger, you let go of the pastor's leg and be on your way." Later his name was shortened to Strange. That dog was nothing if not strange. I have written elsewhere about the crimes and misdeeds of Strange and won't repeat them here. As for a brief description of his true character, revealed shortly after it became clear to him that he had a new home with our family—it is difficult, except perhaps simply to reverse the Boy Scout Law. He was untrustworthy, disloyal, unhelpful, unfriendly, offensive, rude, etc. As a Boy Scout, I found these characteristics to be particularly offensive, even in a dog. Perhaps it was Strange who created in me a reluctance ever to become a true dog person. The half-dozen or so other dogs I've owned off and on over the years have not in any way eased that reluctance. For the most part, though, I have enjoyed their company and grieved at their passing, which, in a couple of cases, at least, seemed not quite soon enough.

There is a big difference between being a dog owner and a dog person. My friend Dan is a dog person. Dogs are such a big part of his life that without a dog he would be somebody else entirely. I wouldn't even recognize him without dogs. By contrast, you could take away my dog, Clarence, and not notice any difference in me at all, except maybe I couldn't stop smiling. "He's all yours," I'd say. "Have a good time with him. Just keep the fly rods out of his reach and you'll learn to love him."

If you want to know what a true dog person is like, you should meet my friend Dan. When his dog, Peat, got too old to hunt, Dan would take him out to a grouse woods and carry him around, just so the dog could sniff the air. True dog persons are usually pretty nice guys.

For some unknown reason, a television producer, also by the name of Pat, decided he wanted to do a TV show of me out in the woods hunting grouse. Since I am supposedly a humor writer, I tried to introduce a little comedy into the show by missing every shot. Although Dan and Pat appreciated this hilarious comedy, Peat couldn't conceal his disgust, if shaking his head in apparent disbelieve is any indication. Well, no matter how smart a dog is, you can't expect him to appreciate humor.

finding My Roots

A while back, my wife, Bun, read a disarming little book on how to collect and prepare wild foods, and ever since then we've been more or less living off the land or, more accurately, out of the swamp. This is not nearly as easy as it may sound, and the reader contemplating trading his grocery cart for a bucket and a pair of hip boots may profit from my experience.

At first, grubbing for groceries directly from the ground was not my idea of a fun weekend, but after a few outings to field, forest, and swamp, I came to abhor it. Nevertheless, Bun's impenetrable logic eventually drove me to take up in earnest the little-known avocation of foraging.

"You should know such things," Bun would say, "just in case."

Her phrase, "just in case," as she well knows, never fails but to fill me with dread. I instantly envision the Four Horsemen of the Apocalypse riding hell-bent through the front door, scaring the wits out of the rather amiable wolf who hangs out there.

Thus motivated, I rushed to the library and checked out every wild food book in sight, not to mention *Wildflowers of the Pacific Northwest* and *The Wonderful World of Insects* (one never knows). That, by the way, happens to be one of Bun's favorite expression—one never knows. And, indeed, he or she doesn't. Otherwise he or she would never take up foraging as a hobby.

Plants and animals that I previously had thought to be merely innocent weeds and rodents were described in these books as being extremely tasty. This was true. They did have a great deal of taste.

Before long, my reputation as a wild food expert had spread through the neighborhood. Charlie Spivak had done most of the spreading, my foraging efforts fitting nicely into his humorous repertoire.

Charlie and I were hiking in the mountains one day when I spotted a small broad-leaf plant growing among some rocks.

"Miner's lettuce," I said authoritatively.

"Good to eat?" Charlie asked.

"Try some." I gave him my prepare-yourself-for-a-real-treat smile.

Charlie insisted that I try some first, another example of the lack of trust among people nowadays.

I popped in a leaf and began to chew, Charlie staring expectantly at me. The leaves, whatever kind they were, had what might be described as a delayed taste, which, when it finally arrived, went off in my mouth like a small bomb of bile.

"Aaaaa!" I said calmly. "Now here is a good example of what miner's lettuce isn't. Let this be a lesson to you, Charlie."

About this time I became aware that wild food proponents have their own definition for the word "edible." To them, "edible" means any food that won't kill you. The possibility of killing the person who fed it to you goes unmentioned.

Consequently, the neophyte wild food forager soon learns to limit his wild food diet to those flora labeled in the books as "choice." Many of the fungi known as toadstools are actually mushrooms. There are many old wives' tales about how to tell a wild mushroom from a poisonous one. These should be avoided. Perhaps you have noticed how few old wives are around these days. The only surefire test for wild mushrooms is simply to eat one. If you are still alive the next day, that was probably an edible mushroom. If absolutely nothing happens the next day, you are probably dead. Mushrooms producing this result are probably toadstools.

Wild food foraging provides some excellent conversation-openers. One day I was standing next to a tall, nervous chap at a bus stop in one of our rougher sections of town. As is my habit, I was studying the vegetation in the vacant lot behind us. I had done so often before but had never detected anything edible. Suddenly, I saw it—a patch of wild burdock! In my excitement, I pointed and yelled at the man, "Look! A bunch of wild burdock!"

The man dropped his briefcase and took off running. This just goes to show how uptight so many of our urbanites are becoming nowadays. They should try to mix a little wild food in with their diets.

The Longest Three Miles

Our little family farm was located exactly three miles north of Sandpoint, Idaho, on U.S. Highway 95, known in those days as the Bonners Ferry Highway. Because of that, all my life I have been able to estimate a distance of three miles almost exactly. I have never been able to estimate anything else requiring math with any degree of accuracy, but ask me anything requiring an estimate of three miles and I will nail it. I believe that is because so much of my early life, at least until I went off to college, took place on those three miles. It was said of Mongol warriors that their home was the back of a horse. It might have been said of my teenage friends and me along the Bonners Ferry Highway that our home was the seat of a bicycle. My longest trip over those three miles, however, by my estimate at the time, lasted about a month. But I was only about five years old. First, however, I must tell you about our little farmhouse.

My earliest memory, at about age two, consisted of my wandering around in the backyard. I had taken off all my clothes and was stark naked. Our free-range family chickens wandered with me, clucking all the while in a somewhat puzzled manner, if my recollection is correct. At one point I came to a large pan of water, apparently set out by my grandmother or mother for the chickens to drink. I climbed into it and sat down. The water was warm and comfortable. I remember that sensation distinctly. The chickens seemed quite offended. They gathered around the pan, clucking in an excited manner, apparently expressing some chicken form of outrage, never before having had a naked person sit down in their drinking water. Suddenly, my grandmother tore out of the house, snatched me from the pan, and raced back in the house. As I was told many years later, Gram had spotted some visitors coming down the driveway and didn't want them to see a member of the family sitting naked in a pan of water out in the yard. Gram had a stroke a few days later, and I and my chicken-pan venture were blamed for it. She lived for another fifty years, however, and I never got any credit for those.

Some time ago, I came across an old family photo of the house. It was a rather cute affair, partially enclosed by a white picket fence overgrown with wild roses. The photo didn't show a large cedar stump in the backyard, but I know it was still there at the time the photo was taken. That cedar stump was the cause of the longest ride I have taken in my entire life, and I have been to and back from Europe and the Orient several times. None of those trips was anywhere near as long or as pleasurable as that six-mile roundtrip at about age five that I took to and from Sandpoint with my father.

One day, Dad said to my mother, "I think I'll dynamite that big cedar stump in the backyard."

My mother said, "No, Frank, don't do it! You know nothing about dynamite or dynamiting!"

"Ha!" Dad responded. "How hard can it be?"

I don't recall the exact words of the argument but I seem to recall it was long and heated.

At one point, Mom probably pointed out that Dad had wrecked the family car after a night spent partying with some of his friends. In any case, Dad no doubt responded by saying he would hitch up our team of horses to our farm wagon, drive them to town, pick up a box of dynamite, return home, and dynamite the stump.

Mom said, "Well, you'll have to take Pat with you."

No doubt this prolonged the argument, but eventually Dad agreed to take me along on the wagon trip to town to pick up the box of dynamite.

Let me state right up front that driving to town on the rough board seat of a farm wagon stretches those three miles to a distance beyond human comprehension, at least to a five-year-old human. I'm not sure how old I was when we left but I was about eighty when we returned. When we finally got to town, Dad bought the box of dynamite and set it on the wagon, which was parked at the curb on one of the main streets of downtown Sandpoint, apparently with no worries in the world that it might be stolen. I guess Sandpoint at the time was populated only by extremely honest persons or at least persons who didn't need a box of dynamite. Then Dad took me by the hand and led me to a business establishment across the street. It was the most interesting place I have ever visited, and I have wished all my life I could find one like it.

All the people there were having a wonderful time, and every one of them seemed to know my father and to be his friend. Dad introduced me all around, then picked me up and set me on this long table-like contraption I think was called "the bar." The man behind the bar set a large mug of beer in front of my father and a bottle of pop in front of me, and the wonderful time started, with Dad telling stories and everybody laughing themselves sick, and the bar man renewing our drinks whenever they ran out. After a while, we left the establishment, climbed back on the wagon, and headed home. The ride back seemed a lot shorter than the ride to town, something less than an eternity anyway. Dad said, "Let our visit to the bar be our own little secret, OK?"

"You bet," I said. I could hardly wait to grow up. I'd had no idea grownups had these secret places where everybody was happy and shouted and joked and had a wonderful time.

The next day Dad prepared to blow up the giant cedar stump.

Mom supervised the operation. "Good heavens, Frank!" she exclaimed. "How many sticks have you put under the stump now?"

Dad told her a number.

"Good heavens!" she said again. "I think that's way too many."

"It's an awfully big stump," Dad said. "I'll put in a few more sticks, just to be on the safe side."

Finally, he lit the fuse and he, Mom, and I ran out into the middle of our hayfield. I don't recall exactly how far that was but it wasn't far enough. I still have dreams about . . . well, I won't go into that.

We waited and waited for the dynamite to go off. "Maybe something happened to the fuse," Dad said, or something like that. "Maybe it went out. I should go check—!"

KA–BAMMMM!

That giant cedar stump rose straight up in the air like a rocket taking off for the moon. It sailed over the top of the house and came crashing down on the white picket fence. That is how I know the stump remained in the backyard when the photo was taken. The picket fence was still there.

Scrabble's Powers of Observation

Even as I piloted my classy new pickup truck into my driveway, I could feel Scrabble's eyes on me, a disgusting sensation if there ever was one. He was undoubtedly manning the observation post in his domicile across the street, said observation post being equipped with the most advanced and sensitive electronic surveillance gear for the detection of any new purchase I happened to make. I turned off the purring engine, leaped out, and sprinted for my front door, but too late. Scrabble had already streaked across the street and cut me off . . .

"Wait up a sec!" he shouted breathlessly. "I see—*gasp*—you got yourself a—*gasp*—new truck."

I slid to a stop and shrugged in acceptance of defeat. Scrabble would have gotten to me sooner or later anyway. Still, it would have been nice to enjoy my new truck defect-free for another hour or two.

"Nice paint," Scrabble said.

"Thanks," I said.

"I thought about buying one of these myself," he went on, "until I found out they have a lot of problems with the cranker points. That wouldn't be a problem, of course, if they was covered by the warranty, which they ain't. Costs about $18,000 to have your cranker points replaced. But that's not the big problem."

"What's the big problem?"

"The gunker welds. They tend to bust at any speed over thirty-five, and the engine falls out and goes skittering down the highway. Oh, I see they're still equipping these trucks with Zop headlights. They're OK, but the only way you can buy replacements is by trekking into a remote village in the Himalayas, where local craftsmen build them by hand and sell them only after you have proved your worthiness by walking barefoot over a hot bed of coals."

OK, so I'm exaggerating, but you get the idea. As far as I know, Scrabble doesn't have a job. He may have had one once, but I think the stress of worrying that I might buy something while he was away at work proved too much for him and he retired on disability. He now seems in perfect health, thanks to the miraculously recuperative powers derived from his critiquing not only any new purchase I happen to make but also my existing possessions.

Explosions are a specialty of Scrabble's. Any product I buy powered by gasoline has a history of killing or maiming several dozen people, not the least of whom is the object's owner. Despite the fact that none of my machines have ever exploded, Scrabble has instilled in my mind that potential. Every time I start a gasoline motor, I have the vague feeling I may be igniting a fuse. Several other neighbors have commented on my tendency to leap back whenever I pull the starter cord on my lawn motor. "It's just a precaution," I tell them. Scrabble, by the way, doesn't live across the street from any of them.

If I show up with a plastic bag containing a few groceries, Scrabble rushes over. "I see you're using one of them plastic bags. You know they don't disintegrate for three million years and are starting to clog up all the oceans."

If I show up with a paper bag, I learn from Scrabble that every day a forest the size of Vermont is cut down to make paper bags.

Lately, I've taken to carrying groceries home concealed in my clothes.

"Where's the tomato sauce?" my wife asks.

"Right here in my inside vest pocket. Why do you ask?"

"And the box of cornflakes?"

"Tied to my chest, where else?"

The criterion for engaging Scrabble's critical scrutiny seems to be only that I possess the object. I've owned a fine little outboard motor for upward of ten years. Unlike most of the hundred or so machines I've owned, the outboard actually runs. Indeed, it has never failed me. One rip of its starter cord and it purrs like a kitten. It will hum along all day long on a couple pints of gas. I love that little motor.

"Uh-oh," Scrabble said, peering into my garage. "You got yourself one of those little outboard motors.

"Yes," I said triumphantly, "and it has served me impeccably for over ten years. So what do you think of that, Scrabble?

"Excellent motors," he replied.

"Really? You mean my motor has the Scrabble seal of approval?"

"Yes, indeed. I assume you have never once heard it ticking."

"Ticking? No, I don't believe I have."

"Good," he said. "Just to be on the safe side, though, you might want to listen for a ticking sound. If you hear it, you might want to shut the motor off instantly."

Only once afterward did I think I heard a ticking sound coming from the motor. I had to laugh at my own reaction to Scrabble's outrageous powers of suggestion. I calmly picked up an oar and used it to push the off button.

A while back I managed to sneak home a new suit without Scrabble's detecting it. I actually don't wear the suit that much, not that I'm worried Scrabble will see me in it and rush over to point out its defects. It's mostly because I haven't been able to discover why it makes that slight ticking sound.

The Dark and Other Dangers

A young fellow recently wrote to tell me that he and some of his friends had been thinking about sleeping out in his backyard. He wanted to know if I had any advice for them. I did. Since the age of eight, I have slept out in backyards, although not for quite a few years now. Sleeping out in the backyard is the kid's version of Peary going to the North Pole, Amundsen to the South Pole, Livingstone to Africa, and McManus to the backyard. I must admit in all modesty that the adventures of those other explorers dim to insignificance compared with mine.

It is my belief that the proper location of the heart of any true explorer is in the throat. I say this based on my own experience of spending a night out alone in the backyard. The fact that those other adventurers failed to mention this significant fact makes me suspicious of the veracity of their various written accounts.

I don't recall the specific date of my outing, but I probably could look it up on the Internet. It was the longest night in the history of the world, so I shouldn't have trouble finding it.

Why did I put myself through this ordeal? Why does any explorer? It is in our blood to venture forth and probe the unknown. For me, the backyard at night constituted the great unknown. It fairly begged for discovery. Also, I had grown sick of school and had made up my mind to become a mountain man. If I could have become a mountain man only in daylight, I would have headed for the mountains like a shot. But there is always an obstacle between the true explorer and the achievement of his ambition. In my case, it was the dark.

I do not mean to imply that up until the age of eight I'd had no experience with the dark. Why, you might ask, didn't my mother provide my room with a night light? To even ask that question would identify your parent as a member of the Wimp Generation. Had I even raised the question of a night light, Mom would have laughed so hard she might have hurt herself, and I certainly didn't want to be responsible for that. Admittedly, the dark of my room was not voluminous. It was a block-shaped cube of about eight feet. Over the years, I learned to deal with this cube and even came to appreciate its limits.

Outside in our backyard at night, however, dark appeared to have engulfed the whole world, or at least the portion of it that I could see. In its vastness, the outside dark contained wolves, cougars, bears, coyotes, rattlesnakes, bats, poisonous spiders, and nonpoisonous spiders. As a member of the select club of explorers, I could easily imagine Dr. Livingstone getting a little nervous as he looked out of his tent suddenly to see the last strands of daylight being slurped up the trunks of tall trees to disappear into the open maw of night.

As I grew older and started to camp out in the mountains with a little group of friends, I was pleased to detect a fear of the dark in at least one of them. We slept out in the open air, exposed to the dark every night. On at least one occasion, a kid I'll call Homer suddenly stopped unrolling his sleeping bag as night closed in around us. Then he stuffed the sleeping bag back in his pack and without even bothering to say "Goodbye," disappeared back down the trail we had come up. His early arrival home apparently caused his parents to think he might be afraid of the dark. So they bought him a little white tent, just big enough for the four of us to sleep wedged in side by side.

That tent was a great comfort to me. Sure, it got dark inside at night but it was a tiny cube of darkness, something I found easily manageable.